Life's HIGHEST Delight

*Delighted to serve with
you in Christ' service*

Ron Williams

12-12-97

Life's HIGHEST *Delight*

Understanding the Person & Passion of God

RON WILLIAMS

Dedication

To my wife, Carole, and my family:

    Scott, Dana, Kyle, Hannah, Mark, Lynn,

    Grace, Derek, and Sonia

who have made my life full, and who have

been my greatest encouragers to write.

Contents

Foreword

It was a refreshing October getaway—a reprieve from weeks of intense demand and fulfilling ministry. As Anna and I drove through rustic back roads of the mid-American setting, we savored the mix of melancholy and magnificence of autumn. Spread like apple butter across toast, the panorama of the Indiana countryside was a blend of both bitter and sweet. Like the luscious spread of the apple's tartness and the smooth texture of butter, there is a satisfaction to the senses as well as to the emotions.

During this October breakaway, another couple joined us who had never visited this area where we spent some of our earlier years of ministry. With the "knowing" of veterans at the Inn's table, we angled our course across Hoosier highways to the little village of Nashville in Brown County. The scenery increased in vividness. We also wanted to introduce them to a certain eatery's food fare that would qualify for every "Scrumptious award" offered anywhere. The reason? Taste-fulfilling satisfaction!

Whether in the eye or on the taste buds . . . seeing the scenic or sampling the scrumptious food . . . we can identify with experiences of *sensory* satisfaction. We know the fullness and the rich experience of the beauty of creation around us or of a delectable meal inside us. Now with these senses awakened, I invite you to sense transcending satisfaction—a multi-dimensional satisfaction that can encompass your whole being.

The invitation is to "see" by looking at a chapter or two in this book. I believe you will be hooked by a rich table of fulfillment prepared by one who has tasted the flavors of experience he shares on these pages.

In the following pages, Ron Williams describes satisfaction at deeper and broader arenas of life than our surroundings can ever provide. I first met Ron Williams in Los Angeles while he was studying for the ministry to which God had called him and his dear wife, Carole. Our first meeting involved an assignment to write youth materials—part of my task as national youth director for the Foursquare Churches in North America. Even at that preliminary stage of Ron's evolving ministry, I observed great potential and promise in this young man's life. The passage of years has not dimmed the brightness of those prophecies. Ron and Carole Williams are regarded as pillars of strength wherever they serve. They are more than *gifted,* they are *godly.*

Let me quickly explain what I mean by godly. Many of us observe people, or settings, described as godly and later discover them to be either stuffy or boorish—something considerably less than "like the Lord." So I reserve my use of it to characterize a person who is going to talk to us about satisfaction.

By *godly* I mean "clear-headed," able to communicate to you with interesting stories, the way Jesus did. I mean "loving," conveying a gentleness of concern for *you,* the way our Father God's loving-kindness flows in, surrounds, and embraces. I also mean "penetrating," entering with warmth and power, the way the Holy Spirit does in bringing us bright blessing and new capacities for dealing with our days, our duties, our dilemmas, and our destiny.

Ron's expansive insight is gleaned from a life of global exposure and intellectual diligence, coupled with a self-sacrificing care for people and their needs. These characteristics qualify him as a *godly* friend and writer, whom I believe you will thank me for introducing to you.

So open this jar of "apple butter" (or substitute your own favorite spread if you're not an aficionado of apple butter)! You are in for a taste of "satisfaction." You will see how true satisfaction involves the blend of life's bitter with its sweet, and how in the hand of God those ingredients bring about the primary thing He created each of us to know: *Fulfillment!*

Yes, that *is* true! God did not create us as instruments for His exploitation. Rather, He created us each to know the highest level of enjoyment and satisfaction within the scope of His unlimited supply. The guidance in His Word and His redeeming gift of life in Christ bring us to taste the joys these unspeakable graces offer. He desires to bring you to life's highest delights—the realizing of *all you were meant to be!*

Ron Williams has written a "cookbook" to show how you and I can find the maximum fulfillment intended for us when we were first conceived in our Creator's mind. So keep reading . . . and "taste and see that the Lord is good" (Psalm 34:8).

Jack W. Hayford
The Church On The Way
Van Nuys, California

Introduction

"Liar!" I accused my reflection in the mirror. A friend had just asked me one of those piercing questions, forcing me to don my ecclesiastical robe of hypocrisy. If I had answered honestly, I would have blown my spiritual cover, or should I say, positional pride. So I gave the expected answer, "Yes, things are going great!" Now, back in the hotel room with no one to confront me but my feelings and God, I stood condemned in my own self-righteousness.

Actually, my friend's question hadn't been all that bad! And he had asked it with genuine concern. *For some reason*, during a brief conversation at the 1994 Foursquare Convention in Sacramento, California, Roger had changed our subject of conversation and asked, "Are you satisfied . . . with what you are doing . . . and with the Lord?"

Inside, something other than my stomach churned, "There's that word again!" *Satisfaction.* The same word convicted me weeks earlier during a church service in Santa Fe Springs, California. That lingering word had haunted me ever since. The recurring word described everything I wasn't.

Satisfaction should describe my nearly 30 successful years in the ministry. I had pioneered a church in Canada, served 16 years as missionary in Hong Kong and Asia,

11

and was now a denominational leader and professor at a Bible college. Satisfaction should characterize the life of someone who had been blessed with a thoughtful and loving wife, three sons all married to believers, and three of the most precious grandchildren of all time—plus many other sons and daughters of the faith in every part of the world. But it didn't. Something was missing.

For the past three years two options had been causing a struggle within me. I knew that soon a decision would be demanded. If the choice had been between good and bad, it would have been easy. But both assignments given me by the Lord and by my denomination were wonderful. One was the opportunity to develop a communications strategy for the International Church of the Foursquare Gospel; the other was the fulfillment of a lifelong desire to train others for the ministry at LIFE Bible College in San Dimas, California. Ever-increasing effectiveness in both areas was putting strain on my ever-increasing age!

Deep inside, I sensed the direction the Lord was leading, and it wasn't my way. On one occasion, I tried to manipulate outcomes to fit *my* perception of what God was calling and gifting me to do. In His immutable way, God caused such attempts to fail. Although I was editor of our denomination's magazine, which was reaching nearly 100,000 homes as well as many churches and institutions, I was miserable and made everyone around me feel the same. I was frustrated and confused.

Now, in front of the mirror, I stood face-to-face with myself, honestly confessing my need for God to do a new work within me. I simply said, "God, I need to hear from You, NOW!"

The pages that follow are not about sin or sacrifice, but about finding satisfaction in the Lord. They are written for believers just like me who, for the most part, have prayerfully and carefully followed the Lord, yet have not found the fulfillment that is part of redemption's gift. As I have revealed my dilemma, I have discovered that if we are honest with ourselves and others, a major portion of God's people experience this lack. The solution is to rediscover who God is, what He really desires, and how we can work out His design in our lives.

The following pages contain word studies, but are not exclusively structured for scholars. Doctrine is discussed, but this book is not written to be read only by theologians. And while testimonies from ministry are given, this writing should never be classified as a ministerial handbook. The purpose is to focus on people like me:

- Believers who, amid all their activity for God, too often forget that Christianity is a relationship

- Believers whose ministry to others always radiates from personal integrity within

- Believers who trust that God's abundant mercies will be bestowed on those who "hunger and thirst for righteousness."

Are you still searching for satisfaction in your Christian walk? If so, this book is for you.

Part I

God's Design

Blessed is the man You choose,
And cause to approach You,
That he may dwell in Your courts.
We shall be satisfied with the Goodness of
Your House, of Your holy temple.

–Psalm 65:4

Put
Down
Your
Paintbrush

"Now" turned out to be three days later. It was the last day of the 1994 International Foursquare Convention I had helped to plan. Dr. Pat Robertson was sharing with the 1,500 plus pastors and leaders of the Foursquare Church how God had directed and expanded the CBN ministry beyond his wildest imagination. In attributing the success in his ministry to the Lord, this anointed servant of God alluded to a recent article he read in *Time* magazine about the restoration of Michelangelo's *Last Judgment* mural on the ceiling of the Sistine Chapel (John Moody, "A Vision of Judgment").

Today experts claim that this fresco of 1,700 square feet combines all the creative genius and techniques of artistry available then. Someone even commented that should the mural be closely examined, every color known to humankind is included. Michelangelo gave five years of his life to creating the masterpiece.

Completing his illustration, Dr. Robertson asked, "How do you think Michelangelo would have reacted if on the last day of his work, a young boy would have entered the chapel, climbed up the scaffolding, pulled out a small can of yellow paint and a brush, and said, 'I like the painting, Mike, but there are a few places that could be improved!'"

I did not hear the speaker's remaining statements. But I did hear a still small voice inside asking, "Ron, how long have I been painting the mural of your life?"

"For over 53 years, Lord." (I was actually 39 years old with 14 years' experience.)

"And who do you *really* want to paint the rest of the mural?"

"You, Lord, of course!"

"Then, why don't you put down your can and brush of preconceived prejudices, plans, and perspectives, and allow Me to complete My masterpiece? Remember, Ron, you are My workmanship, not your own!"

"Put down my paintbrush, eh? Just how do I do it, Lord?"

"Remember what you have been teaching your students? You've told them that the way to be doing My will five years from now is simply to do My will each day. Why don't you just dedicate yourself fully to what I put before you each day and allow Me to work out your future? If you are willing to do so, you will find the satisfaction I've been trying to introduce into your life."

An Honest Answer

As I returned to my responsibilities, I began obeying God's instructions. A series of events began to take shape that led to one of the most important and fulfilling decisions in my life and ministry. Most of all, a sense of satisfaction began to emerge! A few weeks ago my friend repeated the question about satisfaction that he had asked two years earlier. My answer was the same, "Of course I am satisfied with what I am doing and with God." But this time, I was honest.

It is surprising to discover how often the term *satisfaction,* or its equivalent, appears in the writings of David. Listen to his words:

> How precious is Your lovingkindness, O God! Therefore the children of men put their trust under the shadow of Your wings. They are abundantly *satisfied* with the fullness of Your house, and You give them drink from the river of Your pleasures. For with You is the fountain of life; in Your light we see light (Psalm 36:7-9).

> Because Your lovingkindness is better than life, my lips shall praise You. Thus I will bless You while I live; I will lift up my hands in Your name. My soul shall be *satisfied* as with marrow and fatness, and my mouth shall praise You with joyful lips (Psalm 63:3-5).

> Blessed is the man You choose, and cause to approach You, that he may dwell in Your courts. We shall be *satisfied* with the goodness of Your house, of Your holy temple (Psalm 65:4).

Bless the Lord, O my soul; and all that is within me, bless His holy name! Bless the Lord, O my soul, And forget not all His benefits: Who forgives all your iniquities, Who heals all your diseases, Who redeems your life from destruction, Who crowns you with lovingkindness and tender mercies, Who *satisfies* your mouth with good things, so that your youth is renewed like the eagle's (Psalm 103:1-5).

That is nice rhetoric for a harpist, shepherd boy dancing over the hills of Jerusalem! With a naïveté and simplicity understood only by God's "sheep," David penned these wonderful songs.

Wrong! A closer study of these psalms reveals that each of these bold statements about finding satisfaction in the Lord was not made when David was a "shepherd-king-select," reigning on a throne in the City of Zion. In fact, David wrote these when he was hiding in caves throughout Zion's hills from Israel's King Saul who sought to take his life.

The Source of Satisfaction

Satisfaction is not derived from outward circumstances. Satisfaction results from that which is going on within us. Such fulfillment is found . . .

- In the shadow of God's wings
- In His loving-kindness
- In His trustworthiness
- In the goodness of His house
- In our receiving His benefits.

Dyann found the source of satisfaction. Three years ago, she returned home one evening to find her husband had been drinking. The alcohol took its toll on his emotions and volition. Her distraught husband opened the gun cabinet. Fearful of what he might do, Dyann rushed next door to call for help. Dialing 911, she heard the gun shot that took her husband's life. It seemed he had everything going for him—a confession as a believer, a full pension for the rest of his life, two cars and a RV in the front yard, two grown children (both married and fulfilling God's call on their lives), four beautiful grandchildren, and a faithful, loving wife. Now the only thing left was a heritage of guilt and anger.

Six months following the first tragedy, a devastating earthquake struck Southern California. The epicenter was just three blocks from Dyann's house. Though the structure miraculously escaped damage, her cupboards emptied, walls cracked, and she lost her heirlooms. Then just as friends finished repairing and painting the house, a second earthquake opened all the holes and cracks again.

Soon after the earthquakes, Dyann's 89-year-old mother suddenly took ill. Following a brief stay in the hospital, she died. The good news is that during the time in the hospital she acknowledged the Lord to be her Savior.

For most people, any one of the above events would have destroyed their peace and perspective. But Dyann confronted each of these calamities with a joy and satisfaction in the Lord that grew stronger. Yes, there were moments of anxiety, hours of sorrow, and days of adjustment and readjustment. But it was in spite of the troubles, not because of them, that Dyann experienced satisfaction in the Lord.

"Grandma Lam," an energetic 96 year-old woman who

lives in an outlying village in Kowloon, Hong Kong, also found the source of satisfaction. For more than 60 years, she and her husband were pastors. As they grew older, they assisted young pastors who had assumed difficult churches. Her favorite verses were Psalm 103:1-5 and her favorite chorus, "Oh, How Marvelous Our Savior's Love to Me." Above all, she understood spiritual warfare and intercessory prayer long before these topics became techniques in church-growth strategy or a specialized department of the church.

In 1943, the Japanese invaded the British crown colony of Hong Kong. In preparation for their arrival, the Japanese sent two things by air: pamphlets warning the colony's citizenry of the coming invasion, and bombs. Instead of leaving the colony along with multitudes of other people, Grandma Lam elected to remain behind "to pray for the city." It was her conviction that her home, friends, and neighbors needed the covering of prayer. She knew prayer was more effective than any antiaircraft fire.

One evening as she knelt in prayer at her sofa on the third story of her home, there was a loud noise behind her. The interruption did not phase Grandma one bit; she went on praying. An hour or so later, after finishing her time in prayer, she turned to discover a hole in her roof. A bomb had passed through all three floors below and was now imbedded in the foundation of the home—without detonating.

Years later, talking about those difficult days in Hong Kong, she told of thousands who were killed or placed into prison camps and of a time when food was scarce and danger was all about. Grandma Lam always returned to one theme: the loving-kindness of the Lord and the way He renewed her strength "like the eagle's" (Psalm 103:5).

Satisfaction does not mean the absence of tension or struggle; rather it is a confidence that the Lord's lovingkindness and benefits are sovereign in all circumstances. Maybe satisfaction is as near to believers as their remembering His faithfulness.

According to the dictionary, *satisfaction* carries these meanings:

1. Complete gratification

2. The extinguishing of a claim or obligation by payment, performance, restitution, or the rendering of services

3. Atonement or compensation.

Promises of the Word

To *satisfy* is to supply fully what is desired, expected, or needed. It also implies a freedom from doubt or anxiety, resulting in assurance and conviction. This is accomplished by the two parties in an agreement fulfilling the conditions of their promise or giving what is due. The opposite of satisfaction is denial, disappointment, refusal, restraint or starvation.

Applying this definition to the Christian's experience, satisfaction in the Lord is that deep-rooted conviction and assurance that God will complete all the conditions of His promises, no matter what the circumstances. With His willingness and commitment to meet His initiated covenant comes total supply, thereby encouraging our faith in Him and causing us to remember His faithfulness to us. There is no disappointment in Jesus.

In the New Testament, the words *ashamed* or *disappointed* are synonymous. Consider the promises of the Word:

> Therefore, having been justified by faith, we have peace with God through our Lord Jesus Christ, through whom also we have access by faith into this grace in which we stand, and rejoice in hope of the glory of God. And not only that, but we also glory in tribulations, knowing that tribulation produces perseverance; and perseverance, character; and character, hope. Now hope does not *disappoint*, because the love of God has been poured out in our hearts by the Holy Spirit who was given to us (Romans 5: 1-5).

> "Behold, I lay in Zion a stumbling stone and rock of offense, and whoever believes on Him will not be *put to shame*" (Romans 9:33).

> For with the heart one believes unto righteousness, and with the mouth confession is made unto salvation. For the Scripture says, "Whoever believes on Him will not be *put to shame.*" For there is no distinction between Jew and Greek, for the same Lord over all is rich to all who call upon Him. For "whoever calls on the name of the Lord shall be saved" (Romans 10:10-13).

Being "put to shame" carries the connotation "to be overcome, subdued or confounded, i.e., totally confused." An example of the meaning of this word is like riding a horse until it drops. We who believe in Jesus Christ and place our trust in His grace will never be "ridden into the ground." Like Abraham, we will be "fully convinced that what He [God] had promised, He was also able to perform" (Romans 4:21).

God's promises are as sure as His person. There is a difference between presumption and Biblical faith. True Biblical faith never begins with our thinking, but rather with God's. True Biblical faith never initiates action, but responds to what God has already accomplished. Faith never forces God to do anything, but lays hold of His willingness. Faith never relies on our determination, but on His delight. The reason so many believers are dissatisfied with the Lord and their present experience is that they have made themselves, rather than the Creator, to be the center of their universe.

Many years ago a missionary friend told me of his most harrowing experience. He was walking up the path to the porch of his home in eastern Pennsylvania when he heard a familiar voice yell, "Here I am, Dad, catch me!" Instinctively, his arms went out as his eyes glanced skyward, just in time to catch his 7-year-old son who had managed to climb up on the roof and wait for his father so that he might leap into his arms. When asked why, the lad's answer was, "I knew you'd catch me, 'cause you're my dad!" Little did the child realize how close he had come to falling on his face or causing his dad to experience a heart attack!

Presumption always brings disappointment, but trust that allows God to fulfill all the obligations of His covenant with us results in sufficiency . . . and in satisfaction.

Many times I pick up the paintbrush and try to finish the mural myself! Then God allows me to experience something which restores perspective. Again I place the brush back in His hands and become His masterpiece. By the way, He bought the canvas, didn't He?

Study Questions

Chapter 1 ▪ Put Down Your Paintbrush

1. In your own words, write a definition of satisfaction.

2. How should you maintain satisfaction in the midst of turmoil?

3. Is being satisfied related to your will?

4. Describe one of your own "paintbrush" experiences.

5. Is satisfaction a "means" or an "end"?

Chapter 2

Under the
Shadow
of His
Wings

How precious is Your lovingkindness, O God! Therefore the children of men put their trust under the shadow of Your wings. They are abundantly satisfied with the fullness of Your house, and You give them drink from the river of Your pleasures. For with You is the fountain of life; in Your light we see light (Psalm 36:7-9).

In Psalm 36, there is an intriguing phrase: "Therefore the children of men put their trust *under the shadow of Your wings.*" Immediately, my mind travels through the Scriptures to the days just prior to our Lord's death. Matthew 23:37-39 and Luke 13:34, 35 record the lament of Jesus as He approached the Holy City and the site of His cross:

O Jerusalem, Jerusalem, the one who kills the prophets and stones those who are sent to her!

How often I wanted to gather your children together, as a hen gathers her brood under her wings, but you were not willing! See! Your house is left to you desolate; and assuredly, I say to you, you shall not see Me until the time comes when you say, "Blessed is He who comes in the name of the Lord!"

Often, we think of a lament as synonymous with weeping. Jesus did weep over the city of His love, but not as an emotional expression of a broken heart. It was the prophetic pronouncement that because of the rejection of God's promised Redeemer, Israel's inheritance would be desolation and frustration, not delight and fulfillment.

According to the apostle Paul in Romans 11:8-10, the gospel, rather than becoming a table of refreshment to satisfy needs, became a trap of despair. Enemies would overwhelm them. A spirit of stupor would be given to them, and their backs would be bowed with the burden of unbelief.

How far this was from God's original desire! "How often I have longed to gather your children together, as a hen gathers her chicks under her wings, but you were not willing" (Matthew 23:37, *NIV*). In prophesying this, the Lord recalled the ballads of David that highlighted the intimacy of Jehovah with His people. He wanted "the children of men [to] put their trust under the shadow of [His] wings" so that they could find *satisfaction* "with the fullness of [His] house" (Psalm 36:7, 8). Rather, they chose a path devoid of light, life, or enjoyment.

Fortunately, we do not have to follow the path of Israel. To us, His people, God includes the experience of satisfaction in His covenant. That satisfaction is contin-

30

gent on our choices. He has already expressed His will. But just as Israel's stubbornness (Romans 10:21) kept them from their promised inheritance, too often our contrariness—the tendency to do just the opposite of what we know to do—keeps us from enjoying all of the best God has for us.

The Vision

Following a service in Northern Maryland where I shared my testimony, a very stately gentleman approached me. He stated that he had seen a vision of the Lord painting the rest of my life's mural.

Shocked, with some skepticism, I asked him to proceed. He described the Master Painter as He held the brush with an open hand. It was possible for me to take back the brush at any point in time. His willingness to surrender the privilege of painting upon my demand was not an illustration of the Lord's weakness, but of His meekness.

My brother in the Lord finished with the statement, "You know what this means; I don't!" I had to restrain myself to keep from following and begging him to give an interpretation.

As I drove back to the hotel through the magnificent Maryland countryside, the Lord gave me understanding. "Ron, your will was not nullified at Calvary. The completion of your life's mural will be based entirely on your daily choice to allow me the privilege of holding the paintbrush. My hand is open. It's up to you!"

Do you know the problem with living sacrifices? They

keep climbing off the altar! God will go just as far with our lives as we allow Him. He leaves it to us whether or not to hide under the shadow of His wings. The consequences are enormous!

By looking at the place where David includes the phrase "Under the shadow of Your wings," we can learn much about the covenant God offers us.

> I have called upon You, for You will hear me, O God; incline Your ear to me, and hear my speech. Show Your marvelous lovingkindness by Your right hand, O You who saves those who trust in You . . . Keep me as the apple of Your eye; Hide me under the shadow of Your wings (Psalm 17:6-8).

When we are under the shadow of His wings, He is aware that we are there. Certainly there is no time when God is not aware of us. But just as David needed the constant assurance of His full attention—that he was the "apple" (center) of His eye—so do we.

Best Friends

Being a grandpa, I am learning the importance of affirmation and attention. I have given specific instructions to my secretary that telephone calls from my children and grandchildren are highest priority. When they call, I am to be interrupted from whatever I'm doing, unless I am in a meeting or session which nears the definition of "life and death." I am thankful to report that such privilege has never been abused by any of the Williams clan.

This very subject came up on one of those days when everything went wrong. It seemed that the more I tried, the more I failed. The phone kept ringing, demanding my energy and time. Totally frustrated, I told my secretary I was not to be disturbed UNDER ANY CIRCUMSTANCES other than the return of the Lord! I meant it and would pray down the wrath of God upon any intruder!

My self-pity and solitude were suddenly interrupted by the intercom: "Ron, you have a call."

"I thought I told you I didn't want to be disturbed!"

"I know, but I think you will want to take this call."

"No, I won't. Tell them to call back later."

There was a shocking boldness about her next statement. "Take the call. . . . YOU NEED IT!"

Reluctantly, I put the receiver to my ear. It was Kyle, my oldest grandchild, then only 3 years old. His mommy and daddy had taught him how to press the right button on their self-dialing phone to reach me.

"Grandpa, you know what?" Translated into "Williams-talk" that meant, "You'd better listen to what I'm about to say!"

"What, Kyle?"

"You're my best friend! Good-bye!" On the other end of the line, I heard the phone slam back onto the receiver.

Reflecting on this incident, I admitted to myself and to God, "I needed that!" To have the assurance from one of the most loved treasures of my life that I was his best friend turned a gloomy day into a day of gladness! (By the way, because he had my listening ear, my grandson was also delighted.) Tears of joy rolled down the cheeks of this 50-year-old, simply because my grandson chose to remind Grandpa that we are best friends!

God's Full Attention

Hiding under the shadow of Jehovah's wings not only brings joy to His heart, but it is also a reminder to me that I have His full attention and protection.

> Be merciful to me, O God, be merciful to me! For my soul trusts in You; and in the shadow of Your wings I will make my refuge, until these calamities have passed by (Psalm 57:1).

This psalm was written when David fled into the cave of Adullam (1 Samuel 22:1), seeking refuge from the murderous hatred of Saul. During a time of great emotional stress with emotions ranging from fear to discontent to great adulation, the man after God's own heart instructed these lyrics to be set to another of his compositions. The emphasis is that "under the shadow of Jehovah's wings" safety and security may be found. Examine the mixture of tension and trust in his words:

> I will cry out to God . . . who performs all things for me. . . . My soul is among lions . . . Among . . . men who are set on fire, whose teeth are spears and arrows. . . . Be exalted, O God, above the heavens. . . . They have dug a pit before me . . . My heart is steadfast; I will sing and give praise. . . . [Therefore,] I will praise You, O Lord, among the peoples; I will sing to You among the nations (Psalm 57:2, 4-7, 9).

The concept of refuge goes back to ancient Oriental wars. A refuge was a location where soldiers could find rest following a horrifying day of fighting, where the wounded could find shelter and be restored to health, where weapons could be sharpened or repaired, and where plans for the next day's battle could be formulated. Cities were also appointed as places of refuge where those accused of murder or manslaughter could flee until they could stand a fair trial (see Numbers 35:6, 14; Joshua 20:2, 3, 7, 8; 21:13, 21, 27, 32, 38).

The Great Wall

I shall never forget the last week of May 1985. A friend and co-laborer in the Lord, Kurrant Lai, invited me to accompany him on a business trip throughout central and northern China. As I stood on a thousand-year-old bridge built by Marco Polo over the canals of Soochow, I felt so insignificant. Seeing the battlefields of Nanking, sailing the magnificent lake in Hangchou which is associated with many fables, and watching the ships sail in and out of the harbor of Shanghai are all imprinted on my memory. To top it off, we visited Peking (now Beijing) with its Tiananmen Square and the Great Wall of China.

Built over a period of 1,500 years and stretching across nearly 10,000 miles, the Great Wall provided protection from the northern Mongolian tribes. This wonder of the world has seen hundreds of battles and untold casualties of humankind's cruelty. I tried to picture what it must have been like to be a soldier fighting from the top of this unbelievable structure. I also shuddered to think how it must have appeared to the enemy who dared to war against it.

Caught up in the overwhelming awesomeness of the moment, I noticed that built along the wall were wide towers, actual rooms, which my friend translated as "fortresses or refuges."

Suddenly, Psalm 57 came alive. To paraphrase it: "Lord, You are my Refuge. When tired from the daily battles of life, I run to You and find rest, sleep, and refreshment. When I'm wounded by the words of others, or by the stupidity of my own actions and failure, I run to You and find acceptance, instruction, and restoration. When I need new equipping for fulfilling Your will, I run to You and find all I need for life, godliness, and ministry. And when I need Your direction, I run to You and enjoy Your wisdom, with my steps ordered by You."

Finding Refuge

For more than a half century thousands of tourists and historians have visited and examined the Nazi prison of Dachau, located in Northern Bavaria, Germany. During World War II, untold thousands became victims of genetic experimentation. Those who survived the atrocities provided history with descriptions of great torture and horror.

Two years ago some German-speaking friends from Lodi, California, made a journey back to the land of their birth. While there, they visited the site of the concentration camp. Taking great interest in the etchings on the walls of the cells and in the tearstains of those without hope, the wife stopped and called for her husband. There, scribbled in her native tongue were the words, "In the shadow of Your wings, I will take my refuge . . . until these calamities all have passed."

Those calamities have passed. The inscriber of those words remains unknown. Humanity is still inhumane to its own, but the refuge under the shadow of Jehovah's wings is just as available today as it was 50 years ago to that unknown writer in Dachau. Hiding under the shadow of the Almighty assures me of His protection.

Think about it! We have God's attention, His security, His safety, and His refuge. All are included in His package . . . if we choose to unwrap it.

Study Questions

Chapter 2 · Under the Shadow of His Wings

1. Read Romans 11:8-10 and explain how the gospel became a "trap" to Israel.

2. What are the factors that hinder us from receiving the fullness of God's covenant?

3. Do a short word search through the Psalms on the term, *loving-kindness.*

4. How does "being the apple of God's eye" assist in developing your confidence?

5. Describe the balance between tension and trust that is presently at work in your life.

Chapter 3

Songs
in the
Night

Because Your lovingkindness is better than life
. . . I will lift up my hands in Your name. My
soul shall be satisfied . . . and my mouth shall
praise You. . . . Because You have been my help,
therefore in the shadow of Your wings I will
rejoice. My soul follows close behind You; Your
right hand upholds me" (Psalm 63:3-5, 7, 8).

I n his book *Treasury of David*, Charles Spurgeon in-
troduces Psalm 63:

This was probably written while David was
fleeing from Absalom; certainly at the time he
wrote it he was king (verse 11), and hard pressed
by those who sought his life. David did not leave
off singing because he was in the wilderness,
neither did he in slovenly idleness go on
repeating Psalms intended for other occasions;

but he carefully made his worship suitable to his circumstances and presented to his God a wilderness hymn when he was in the wilderness. There was no desert in his heart, though there was a desert around him. We too may expect to be cast into rough places ere we go hence. In such seasons, may the Eternal Comforter abide with us, and cause us to bless the Lord at all times, making even the solitary place to become a temple for Jehovah. (Charles Spurgeon, *Treasury of David*, Vol. 2, p. 65)

The greatest sorrow in the heart of a parent is the rebellion of a son or daughter. Should that child seek to destroy the parents' lives, the sorrow is multiplied many times over. David was called the ruler of Israel, but he was now being ruled by the pain of a dysfunctional family. In the past, he had killed a lion and a bear, he had defeated Goliath, but he had never faced such an enemy as he did at this moment.

Amid the turmoil, he discovered within him a thirst—an insatiable longing and compulsion for the lovingkindness of God. As he lay awake at night (as you and I do at times), David remembered the power and glory of the Lord. Like Job of old, he found that God "gives songs in the night" (Job 35:10).

Nights of Discouragement

As David recalled God's goodness, his lips began to praise, his hands raised in adoration, joy filled his heart, and satisfaction sprang forth into merry notes. In the middle of his struggle, David laid down his self-protectiveness to uncover satisfaction beyond what life itself can promise. How amazing that from the darkest nights of discouragement the brightest blessings emerge!

This was true for Leung Mei Ying, a former reporter for the *Peking Daily*. This Christian woman was marked from the moment Chairman Mao Tse-tung and the Communist regime assumed power in China in 1949. A believer in Jesus since her childhood, Mrs. Leung had taught her children to follow the ways of the Lord. After the first few years of the "Liberation of China," as the Communists called it, her husband was killed, her house was searched on many occasions by the authorities, and her children were severely harassed. Finally, Mrs. Leung was imprisoned for 17 years on a minor charge. Many of the years were spent in solitary confinement.

In 1979, following the new "open-door policy" in China, Mrs. Leung was released from prison. Because of her previous affiliation with the Emmanuel Foursquare Church in Shanghai, she came to Hong Kong to visit us one week before Christmas.

As was our Christmas Day tradition, the Williams family enjoyed worship at our headquarters church. We invited Mrs. Leung to join us. As the congregation sang Christmas carols, tears began to flow down her face. We cried too. None of us could imagine what it was like for this lady to be reunited with her church family after 30 years! We marveled as she joined with the angels in the adoration of the newborn King.

After church we invited her home for Christmas dinner. We gathered around the table filled with Chinese and Western cuisine, singing "Silent Night." After finishing the lyrics, "Jesus, Lord, at Thy birth," our guest remarked, "I haven't heard that song in over a quarter of a century."

Stunned, I asked Mrs. Leung how she had maintained her faith during her imprisonment, especially during the long periods of solitary confinement. She smiled, reached into her bag and pulled out dozens of pages, ripped and ragged on the edges but carefully wrapped.

"You see, Pastor Williams, as a child raised in Sunday school, my teachers helped me memorize Scripture. Oh yes, I didn't want to, and even thought it was a waste of time. But more than four decades later, as I was in my prison cell, not knowing what the next day would bring, the Holy Spirit would wake me. He brought those scriptures back to my memory and gave me melodies to match the meter of the Chinese characters.

"You see these papers? They are my hymnbook, a compilation of those verses God brought to my heart in the depths of despair. Pastor, God really does give songs in the night."

As I carefully held those sacred pages in my hands and later compared them to the Chinese translation of the Bible, there was not one discrepancy between what God had written centuries before and what Mrs. Leung had written in her cell.

Leung Mei Ying had learned, like David, that God's loving-kindness could pierce even a prison wall. Though locked away in solitary confinement, she was not alone. Because God was her help, she could rejoice with a song in the night—in the shadow of His wings.

God's Song

Later on, David remembered another songwriter—

Moses. Most commentators believe that Psalm 91 was written by Moses, the emancipator, and later preserved and included in this eternal songbook by King David himself. Listen to the lyrics:

> He who dwells in the secret place of the Most High shall abide under the shadow of the Almighty. I will say of the Lord "He is my refuge and my fortress; My God, in Him I will trust." Surely He shall deliver you from the snare of the fowler and from the perilous pestilence. He shall cover you with His feathers, and under His wings you shall take refuge; His truth shall be your shield and buckler (Psalm 91:1-4).

At the end of the song (verses 14-16), Jehovah sings back to Moses:

> "Because he has set his love upon Me, therefore I will deliver him; I will set him on high, because he has known My name. He shall call upon Me, and I will answer him; I will be with him in trouble; I will deliver him and honor him. With long life I will satisfy him, and show him My salvation."

Man sings, the stars sing, and now we hear God's song! Note the promise right in the middle of God's aria: "I will *satisfy* him." Where is satisfaction found? Abiding under the shadow of the Almighty, even when that shadow is cast over seemingly hopeless situations.

Heidi Tuomisto

The highway seemed clear as Mom Tuomisto put her

foot to the accelerator the afternoon of May 10, 1985. In the car were her daughters, 6-year-old Nina, and Heidi, an energetic 3-year-old. Suddenly, their world became a cacophony of crushing metal and shattering glass. The car was struck on the rear right side by another vehicle traveling at 45 miles per hour. The impact sent them into a spin, colliding against the curb and propelling little Heidi through the side window into a subdivision sign. The sign consisted of four wooden tiers. Heidi crashed through the third tier, her head and body entangled in the broken boards. She was killed instantly.

As the mother tried to get to her daughter, a nervous gentleman forced her back into the car seat, saying "You can't see this! Stay in the car!" Suddenly, God's hand moved across her countenance, and Mom felt great peace and faith. She got up and moved toward the pile of rubble. People were standing in a semicircle. She heard one man state, "It's too late. She's gone!"

The mother focused on the mass of broken boards and mangled flesh. Her child's right arm was twisted, hanging over one end of a board; her right leg split through the other end of the same board, exposing the bones of her left leg near the ankle. There was no movement or pulse. The mother began to whisper, then shout, "In the name of Jesus!" Those standing about thought she was delirious.

The Miracle

Moments later a miracle occurred. A faint, slow heartbeat was noticed. As Nina joined her mother in prayer, Heidi's neck cracked back into place, and she started moaning.

Heidi was taken to the College of Virginia Medical Center. Initial reports from the trauma room revealed Heidi was in critical condition. Surgery would be needed, both on her brain and her internal organs. The doctors gave the little girl a very bleak chance of survival.

In the X-ray room, a second miracle occurred. As the doctors watched the dye in the CAT scan, pressure was suddenly released from her brain. Then the spleen, pancreas, lacerated liver, kidneys, and both sections of her broken pelvis were totally healed before an operation could be performed. The doctors still gave her little hope because of the severe head injuries.

When Heidi was moved to intensive care, she had 37 tubes in her body, casts on her right arm and left leg, and a bolt in her head to measure the pressure.

Her mother writes: "We placed a Bible at her head and another at her feet. We opened them to Psalm 91 and Isaiah 53 respectively, and requested they not be removed. Every minute with her was spent confessing and singing the Word of God over her."

On the fourth day following the accident, Heidi started experiencing seizures, some of which lasted 12 minutes. Examination showed her brain to be totally damaged. When the parents inquired, they were informed that Heidi would need to remain in intensive care for at least two months, followed by six to eight months in the hospital learning to walk again . . . if she lived. The specialists said she would need successive operations on her crushed elbow until the age of 18.

However, on day 6, Heidi came out of the Intensive Care Unit and began talking. By the ninth day, she was doing puzzles for the therapist, and two days later was released from the hospital. By June 10, 1985, just 30 days following the collision, Heidi's elbow was completely healed—without surgery.

God also placed a new bone in Heidi's leg, and she resumed walking, at first with a limp and her foot curved inward. The parents laid hands on her legs each evening, and God caused the leg to grow out, healing the curve and the limp. Three months later when Heidi saw the doctor again, not only did the neurologist report great improvement in Heidi's brain but the orthopedist was also amazed. He declared that there was no evidence on the final X-rays that Heidi had ever been in an accident.

Eight years later in the summer of 1993, my wife, Carole, and I had the opportunity to minister in Asheville, North Carolina, at a family camp. We arrived on a Sunday evening and prepared for the next day's sessions. As we made our way to the dining hall for a good Southern breakfast of buttered grits and orange juice, we noticed an extremely beautiful young lady walk by us. We remarked to each other about the outstanding features in her face.

Our host asked, "Do you know who she is? Do you remember an article you wrote a few years back in your magazine?" Within two seconds, I was introducing myself to Heidi Tuomisto. How loving and kind our Lord had been to this precious young lady!

By the way, I asked her to tell me her favorite verse. Yes, you've already guessed it! "He who dwells in the secret place of the Most High shall abide under the shadow of the Almighty!"

God's loving-kindness also includes sufficient strength for any task. Looking back to the 63rd Psalm, we find

David promising to "follow close" behind [the wings] of Jehovah, recognizing that the sovereign hand of the Lord will uphold him.

T.E.A.M.

Have you ever considered why a flock of birds flies in a V-shaped formation? Have you ever watched long enough to discover that there is a continual changing of the bird which flies at the point?

The principle is so simple that it is profound. It's called a "T.E.A.M."—Together Each Accomplishes Much. Actually, the point bird cuts through the wind resistance, making it easier for the other members of the flock, and providing greater lift. The constant changing of the leader allows the birds not only to share the load but also to rest so that they can continue their long flight. Their key to sustained stamina is to fly as closely as possible to the bird ahead.

Similarly, David rejoices in the fact that as he puts his trust under the shadow of Jehovah's wings, he finds re-joicing (less resistance) and he is upheld by the Almighty's right hand (greater lift).

A song in the night hours of despair, a sustaining hope along the highway of calamity, and the stamina to make it through every flight of faith are all provided by our Lord's lovingkindness . . . and are designed to create within us satisfaction with God.

Study Questions
Chapter 3 • Songs in the Night

1. How can a "good memory" strengthen your satisfaction during times of stress?

2. Trace the various times Moses drew upon his memory of God's loving-kindness.

3. Read through Psalm 91 and make a list of the benefits of being "under the shadow of His wings."

4. Identify those times in your life when God has come through in seemingly impossible times.

5. How can your relationship with others bring "lift" and satisfaction during hard circumstances?

Redeemed
to Be
Satisfied

Blessed is the man You choose, and cause to
approach You, that he may dwell in Your courts.
We shall be satisfied with the goodness of Your
house, of Your holy temple (Psalm 65:4).

The Hebrew calls Psalm 65 a *shur* and *mizmor*—
a combination of poetry and song, a lyrical
poem. It is the first in a series of four such
poems that follow psalms of pleading and longing. Some expositors believe it was designed to have in-
strumental accompaniment and to be sung for the Day of
Atonement as well as for the Feast of Tabernacles.

The Day of Atonement was the one time of the year
when the high priest entered the Holy of Holies before
the Lord to offer sacrifices for the sins of the nation (see
Leviticus 23:27; 25:9). This day usually occurred during
our month of October and was instituted in recognition

of man's inability to offer full atonement for his own sins (see Hebrews 10:1-10).

The divine design for this most sacred and elaborate ritual, according to Leviticus 16 and Numbers 29, is as follows: The priest purified himself by a ceremonial bath, clothed himself in holy linen garments, and made atonement for himself and other priests by sacrificing a bullock. A goat was chosen and then sacrificed in front of the congregation of Israel. The blood from both the bullock and goat were sprinkled inside the Holy of Holies on the mercy seat. A second goat, called the scapegoat, would be sent into the wilderness. The high priest would, after a second ceremonial bath, change his garments again before making the final offering. As he reappeared before the congregation, there would be great joy and celebration because their sins had once again been covered over . . . but only for another year.

Completion of the Harvest

The people fill the courts of the Temple as the congregation of Israel waits for the high priest to emerge from the Holy of Holies. If he stands before the Lord and lives, their sins will have been forgiven; if he is not found worthy or his sacrifice is unacceptable, Israel will remain in her sins. Their praise *waits,* or is *silent,* in the courtyard. Forgiveness has not yet come. Any minute now, they will know.

The hushed expectation was in reality a loud confession of Israel's awareness of her unworthiness, as well as of her dependency on the vow God had made: "Yes, Lord, You alone can and will provide the propitiation for our sins!" As Edward Leigh wrote in his 1657 *Annotations on the Five Poetical Books of the Old Testament*: "Mercy is not yet come, we expect it: whilst thou art preparing the mercy, we are preparing the praise." (Quoted in *The Treasury of David*, Vol. 2, p. 96.)

The Feast of Tabernacles occurred five days after the Day of Atonement (Leviticus 23:34; Deuteronomy 16:13). Lasting eight days, it marked the completion of the harvest and historically commemorated the 40 years when the children of Israel lived in tents. The last day of the feast marked the conclusion of the yearly process of feasts and was celebrated with great joy.

Psalm 65 begins with this descriptive statement:

> Praise is awaiting You, O God, in Zion; and to You the vow shall be performed. O You who hear prayer, to you all flesh will come. Iniquities prevail against me . . . You will provide atonement for them (vv. 1-3).

Suddenly, the priest appears and the crowd erupts in joyful celebration! Their relationship with Jehovah is restored and their transgressions are covered by blood. No longer is there the threat of Elohim's condemnation. They cry out, "Blessed is the man You choose, and cause to approach You, that he may dwell in Your courts. We shall be satisfied with the goodness of Your house, of Your holy temple" (v. 4). Silent anxiety becomes satisfied adoration of the One who had accepted their representative into His presence.

The occasion was far more than any other celebration; it was the difference between life and death, between hope and helplessness—an eternal decision made by an eternal

God. Can you even begin to imagine the relief on the high priest's face when the day was over?

Our High Priest

But there is even better news for us today! The writer to the Hebrews declares:

> But Christ came as High Priest of the good things to come, with the greater and more perfect tabernacle not made with hands, that is, not of this creation. Not with the blood of goats and calves, but with His own blood He entered the Most Holy Place once for all, having obtained eternal redemption. For if the blood of bulls and goats and the ashes of a heifer, sprinkling the unclean, sanctifies for the purifying of the flesh, how much more shall the blood of Christ, who through the eternal Spirit offered Himself without spot to God, cleanse your conscience from dead works to serve the living God? . . . Therefore, brethren, having boldness to enter the Holiest by the blood of Jesus, by a new and living way which He consecrated for us, through the veil, that is, His flesh, and having a High Priest over the house of God, let us draw near with a true heart in full assurance of faith, having our hearts sprinkled from an evil conscience and our bodies washed with pure water. Let us hold fast the confession of our hope without wavering, for He who promised is faithful (Hebrews 9:11-14; 10:19-23).

What humankind cannot do, Christ has already done! The people of Israel could not accompany the High Priest into Jehovah's presence. However, because of the Cross and Resurrection, not only does our High Priest appear continually before God as our atonement, but He also takes us with Him! We no longer fear the wrath of God; rather, we receive His highest favor and forgiveness. Although this mercy is beyond our wildest comprehension and dreams, nevertheless it is true!

An Exhibition of Love

What a picture of mercy and grace! According to the Epistle to the Romans, when we were without strength (totally helpless), when we were ungodly (everything God isn't), when we were sinners (totally missing the mark), and when we were even God's enemies (opposing Him on every side), God put on an exhibition of love so that we might be justified, reconciled, and satisfied, rejoicing in God through our Lord Jesus Christ! (see 5:6-10).

One of my favorite comedians is Mark Lowery, a marvelous young man of God. In one of his first releases, Mark shared about one of the first services he conducted after giving himself to a full-time ministry that totally relied on faith gifts for support. He had just finished a service at a large church when the pastor approached him with nothing but a handshake, "Praise the Lord, Mark. Come again!" In Mark's own words, he received a "love offering—love, no offering!"

On Mark's way home, not only was his pocketbook hurting, but so was his ego! Looking up toward heaven, Mark shouted, "God, your employee didn't get paid tonight! I can't even eat at McDonald's! I surely deserve more than that!"

At that moment, the Lord whispered into Mark's heart, "Hey, Mark, anything above burning in hell is a privilege." Mark realized that being a youth evangelist was better than what he deserved. Since then, God has greatly blessed this brother and has anointed his unique ministry.

Mercy is God not giving you and me what we deserve! Contrary to what most claim, when I get to heaven I firmly believe that rather than shouting "Glory," I will fall on my face in utter silence unable to find adequate expression to describe God's mercy in my life! Even today, I stand in His courtyard, speechless but saved!

Likewise, grace is God giving you and me everything we don't deserve! He has declared us not only righteous and redeemed, but has also given us access into His presence as His beloved children—even His sons and daughters—joint-heirs with Jesus. We also hear His affirmation, "This is My beloved Son, in whom I am well pleased" (Matthew 3:17). Further, to think of our future brings to our lips the gasp, "Absolutely awesome!" Israel could rejoice on only certain occasions; we rejoice continually!

His Choice

A new thought is introduced in Psalm 65:4. This verse talks about the man God chooses and causes to approach Him in His courts. It appears that our approach to God began with Him—it was His choice, not ours.

I vividly remember the Sunday morning in 1953 when I knelt at the altar at the end of the service in Downey, California. Reverend Glenn Campbell and Mr. John Hiatt were kneeling beside me and sharing with me the promises of salvation. It was my decision to walk the aisle that day. I chose to follow Jesus. I went to church that morning as the "whoever" in John 3:16 and returned home for Sunday dinner as the "believer" in John 3:18. I have no doubt that it was my choice. I had exerted the prerogative of my free will.

But it was not my choice alone! For as I began to grow in the knowledge of the Word of God, I discovered John 15:16:

> You did not choose Me, but I chose you and appointed you that you should go and bear fruit, and that your fruit should remain, that whatever you ask the Father in My name He may give you.

> I also read that the God and Father of our Lord Jesus Christ, chose us in Him before the foundation of the world, that we should be holy and without blame before Him in love, having predestined us to adoption as sons by Jesus Christ to Himself, according to the good pleasure of His will, to the praise of the glory of His grace, by which He made us accepted in the Beloved (Ephesians 1:4-6).

God chose me not because He had to, but because He wanted to! He chose me not to the exclusion of others, but to the inclusion of *me*. He chose me not because of what I deserved, but because of His delight. Above all, He chose me not because of how I could benefit Him, but in order to bless me!

As the psalmist writes, "[I] shall be satisfied [never lack] with the goodness [merciful and gracious blessings] of Your house. . . ."

The Election of God

The remainder of Psalm 65 records the blessings God will send upon the earth, causing both the creation and the creature to shout for joy. However, it all begins with the election of God!

As I look at the times I have become dissatisfied with the Lord, I recognize that it is when I have taken for granted the price Christ paid for me. Somehow, I convince myself that God deserves me, that being saved is my right rather than His gift. I send God a "bill" for the cost of my discipleship, and I become very ungrateful . . . until I remember that He redeemed me. Redeemed me to be satisfied!

Study Questions
Chapter 4 ▪ Redeemed to Be Satisfied

1. What spiritual realities did the Day of Atonement and the Feast of Tabernacles preview for today's believer?

2. What lesson does the phrase, "Thou art preparing the mercy, we are preparing the praise" convey?

3. In your own words, define the relationship between mercy and grace.

4. Recall your own conversion experience, the circumstances surrounding it, and the people God used to bring you to Him.

5. How does the fact that God "chose" you bring you to fuller satisfaction?

Crowned
With
Goodness

You who are the confidence of all the ends of the earth . . . You make the outgoings of the morning and evening rejoice. You visit the earth and water it, You greatly enrich it . . .You crown the year with Your goodness, and Your paths drip with abundance (Psalm 65:5, 8, 9, 11).

Our last chapter began by stating that Psalm 65 was a lyrical song sung on the Day of atonement. What a blessed realization to know that not only did we choose the Creator but that the Creator also chose us, even before time existed. Then to be forgiven on top of that . . . !

Song of Celebration

According to traditionalists, the song of celebration was

also sung at the Feast of Tabernacles. This time of celebration began five days after the Day of Atonement (Leviticus 23:34; Deuteronomy 16:13) and lasted seven days. It marked the completion of the harvest. The people of Israel gathered to live in tents, reminding themselves of God's provision to their forefathers during the wilderness wanderings. The climax of the feast signified that the harvest had been completed and rest was now their portion. It was a time to declare, "You crown the year with Your goodness" (Psalm 65:11).

The term *crown* literally means "to encircle, encompass, or surround." From the beginning to the end, God became their source, their confidence, and their destiny. The same term is used by David in Psalm 103:4, 5, when he rejoices over the Lord "Who crowns [encircles] you with lovingkindness and tender mercies, who satisfies your mouth with good things, so that your youth is renewed like the eagle's." This word reminds us of the pillar of cloud by day and the pillar of fire by night which went before in guidance and, when needed, stood behind to deliver the people of God.

The Feast of Tabernacles also typified the future "harvest" from all nations which will be gathered into the City of God to celebrate God's faithfulness in completing that which He has begun.

Promise Fulfilled

"Ron, I have something to tell you," was the way my mother began her story that muggy evening in June 1965. I had just graduated from LIFE Bible College, and the next morning my wife, Carole, my 2-year-old son, Scott, and I would point our 1963 Falcon towards Vancouver, British Columbia, to pioneer a new Foursquare church.

My mother continued, "As you are aware, you were born late in my life. You were born on your oldest sister's 19th birthday, and your other sisters were 17, 15, and 13 years old.

"When I learned I had conceived, I went to a prayer meeting at the Third United Brethren Church in Decatur, Illinois. I knelt at the altar, with several others praying with me. In their presence I promised the Lord that if He would grant me a son, I would return him, just like Hannah did Samuel, to serve in the temple of the Lord. Tonight, nearly 26 years later, that promise has been fulfilled."

We did go to Canada and, a little more than four years later, were appointed as Foursquare missionaries to serve in Hong Kong. It was not without significance that we were commissioned for missionary service during the 1969 International Foursquare Convention, held that May in Decatur, Illinois, less than a mile from where my mother had made that commitment in February 1940.

As hands were being laid upon our family— now including our second son, Mark—I looked to the back of the auditorium. Standing there was an older gentleman by the name of John Slosser, who was failing in his endeavor to maintain composure. You see, he was one of those who witnessed my mother's prayer and was now seeing her promise fulfilled before his eyes.

What a journey had transpired, taking me from my mother's dedication to my own. At the age of 5 days, I was given a short "Life of Christ" Bible. Each Sunday for the next nine years, Pastor Jesse Cotherman would wait until he could see my small Bible before continuing the service. As a matter of fact, until his death in 1983, a day did not pass without Jesse's mentioning my name personally before the throne of grace. Think of it, 43 years—that's more than 15,000 days!

The Teacher

A number of people in my family actively served in World War II. The ending of that war signaled a tremendous shift for us. Believing that the West Coast afforded "golden" opportunities, the majority of our family, including my parents and me, moved to California. Following a time of cultural adjustment and during a time when we could not find a friendly church, a lady in the trailer park where we lived invited me to Sunday school. There, the smile of a teacher touched me so strongly that I had my parents visit the church the next week. That day marked the beginning of four generations of the Williams family who would worship in Foursquare churches—the denomination of which I would become a member of its Board of Directors 39 years later. It was no *coincidence* that I would be taught in Sunday school by teachers who were Bible students, training as ministers and missionaries.

Running From the Lord

Then there were my years of rebellion. Questioning all those core values my parents instilled in me, I tried to run from the Lord during my later high school days. Was it a *coincidence* that in my 1958 school yearbook, a friend *just happened* to write two verses of scripture, Proverbs 3:5, 6? These verses so haunted me that one year later I once again acknowledged the ways of the Lord. Was it pure *coincidence* that I was brought back to the Lord through leading another backslider to repentance? Yes, jealousy resulted in justification!

Was it a *coincidence* that I joined the Air Force and, just several weeks following my renewal to the Lord, was sent to Japan and other parts of Asia? Was it a *coincidence* that I was trained as a linguist, that I visited Hong Kong and actually ate lunch in the same room that a decade later was to become my office? Was it a *coincidence* that I was the only U.S. serviceman released from the Armed Forces during August 1961, when Laos was invaded? My release was made possible because of my enrollment into seminary. Was it only *coincidence* that I would marry a girl who shared the same call God had given me? My life has been full of these *coincidences*!

Such *coincidences* have also impacted the lives of others. In 1959, was it *coincidence* that led my parents to send seven newly published Thompson Chain Bibles to my servicemen friends? One of these Bibles was given to a friend, Harold Dollar, who would become a missionary to Haiti and, later, a faculty member of the missions panel at Biola University.

That Bible would also be used by Harold to lead another serviceman, Bobby Clinton, to Jesus. Dr. Bobby Clinton would later develop the outstanding Leadership Emergence Studies at Fuller Theological Seminary, training and mentoring untold numbers of ministers and missionaries personally, and touching multiplied thousands more through his writings. As a matter of fact, Dr. Clinton was one of my teachers who led me through a Leadership

Emergence Study that traced how the Lord *happened* to show up in every aspect of my 50 years on earth. I discovered anew that the Lord had a marvelous destiny for me.

God's Faithfulness

Listen to some of the principles derived from the rehearsal of God's faithfulness:

1. An awareness by a parent of *God's claim* over his or her child will assist in careful stewardship of rearing that child.

2. The theology of a leader will be greatly influenced by *early images* at home.

3. Effective leaders must realize their *relevance* to the time in which God has placed them.

4. *Models* are of tremendous value in the formation of leadership perception.

5. Good leaders will be sensitive to the *timing and context* for which they are responsible.

6. Effective leaders will always recognize the *providence and preeminence of God* in the situations they face.

7. When a leader remains faithful, *God turns* negative events into positive lessons and growth.

8. A leader will leave room for *divine intervention* in daily experiences.

9. The true affirmation of the credibility of leaders will be the *faithfulness of God* in their lives and works.

10. Effective leaders recognize God's *sovereignty* in the times and seasons He has set for certain persons and even communities.

11. God *sovereignly links* particular leaders together whose relationships over a lifetime of ministry mutually supply what the other lacks.

12. At times, leaders will be asked to *risk their faith* in order to see extraordinary works of God accomplished.

13. Effective leaders recognize that *all promotion* comes from the Lord as a result of faithfulness.

14. True Biblical eldership or leadership always emanates out of *being,* as opposed to *achieving*.

Of the 56 principles derived from the study, 25 percent have to do in some way with the sovereign faithfulness of God in shaping a sense of destiny in my life. And coming to its conclusion, I wrote the following:

> God had been shaping my communication and supervisory skills, even in my teen years. I knew He had been faithful, but had never seen just how determinate God had been in the step-by-step developments. From hence, I will ever be looking at His working in my life with a "period" overview, rather than in an immediate, individual event context.

God's faithfulness in the past is only a deposit on His continued faithfulness in the future. As David recalled the faithfulness of God to His creation, he used the term *confidence.* You and I can surrender control of our destinies to the Lord because He is loyal to His Word and faithful in all His ways. Whom He has called, He is faithful to conform to His image. Whom He visits, He crowns (encircles) with goodness. There are no *coincidences* in the steps of a righteous man or woman—just the crowning of the Lord.

He whom God encircles will shout and sing for joy! He or she will be satisfied, crowned with God's goodness.

Study Questions

Chapter 5 • Crowned With Goodness

1. When you hear someone say, "You have a destiny," what picture comes to mind?

2. From your life experiences, identify major turning points and phrases. What does God's past processing say about the way you will process future decisions?

3. How does God multiply the influence of our witnessing and acts of Christian service?

4. What role does praying for others play in our becoming satisfied?

5. From the principles identified by the author, choose four which apply to your present circumstances.

Chapter 6

Created
With a
Passion

O Lord . . . You have hedged me behind and
before, and laid Your hand upon me. . . . Where
can I go from Your Spirit? . . . For You formed
my inward parts . . . and in Your book they all
were written, the days fashioned for me, when
as yet there were none of them. . . . Search me,
O God . . . and lead me in the way everlasting
(Psalm 139:4, 5, 7, 13, 16, 23, 24).

This morning, I held my one-month-old grand-
daughter, Grace, in my arms. She and her
mother have come to spend some time with us
while Daddy is at camp, ministering to the youth
of their church. Actually, Grace is our third grandchild,
but as every grandpa and grandma well knows, love is
not divided among the grandkids. A grandparent's love
is miraculously big enough to go around equally.

As my scarred, bearded face caressed her soft cheeks, I remembered the events of another morning in June 1995. Grandma and I had been trying to get some sleep in the waiting room of the hospital while my son, Mark, helped his wife, Lynn, through the final hours of labor. At 3:30 a.m., however, Mark appeared at the door. With great anxiety, he informed us that the baby was in trouble. Although the heartbeat was reasonably strong, there was no other movement. A cesarean section would be performed immediately, but there was a chance the baby would not make it. For the first time in my 30 years of ministry, I knew firsthand the feeling parents face when the pregnancy produces a stillborn child.

Scared, Mark, Carole, and I joined hands and proclaimed the promises of God. His mother and I assured our son that the Lord would walk with him and Lynn through whatever took place, and we would be there as well. He returned to the labor room, while we prayed. Nearly an hour later, our 8 pound, 9 ounce, Grace arrived.

Later that morning during breakfast, I leaned over to the new dad and asked, "Mark, this morning when you first heard that Grace might not make it, how did you feel? Wouldn't you rather have given your life than for her to miss her chance at it?" Hearing his "You bet!" I then commented, "Maybe that's the way God felt when He sent His Son. Could it be that He'd rather die than have us do so? He wanted us to have a chance at life."

People of Passion

Each time I think back on both that morning and the

gift of our Savior, I become passionate. Not passionate in the self-glorification and self-gratification of today's "impassioned" society but passionate with eager anticipation, ardent affection, and willingness to endure suffering in order to embrace those things I cherish most.

Whether or not we admit it, all of us are people of passion. We were glued to our television sets, watching the firemen and rescue workers search through the debris to find and free the victims of the May 14, 1995, bombing of the Alfred P. Murrah Federal Building in Oklahoma City. There have been times when each of us remained full of faith, persevering through great difficulties.

To the intellectuals who believe in analyzing everything, I say there are some things simply to be lived, not learned in a book. To those who base their entire lives on their feelings, there is a difference between emotionalism and being emotional. But to those who claim that emotional response is fanaticism or extremism, I remind them that one can be passionate and still maintain balance and self-control. Believe me, as I watched our son almost claw the door down to the hospital nursery, I recognized pure passion. (Pure passion was still there—maybe in greater balance—the first time he struggled through changing Grace's overflowing diaper.)

Song of Passion

Psalm 139 is a song of passion—not only of our passion for God, but also of His passion for us! The shepherd-king songwriter is not just *chasing* after intimacy with the One who made him, but David is fully aware that God, even more so, pursues us. God really loves us!

Emotions fill the entire psalm. George Gilfillan (1813-1878) is quoted in *The Treasury of David* by Charles H. Spurgeon in the following passage:

> Here the poet inverts his gaze, from the blaze of suns, to the strange atoms composing his own frame. He stands shuddering over the precipice of himself. Above all is the All-encompassing Spirit, from whom the morning wings cannot save; and below, at a deep distance, appears amid the branching forest of his animal frame, so fearfully and wonderfully made, the abyss of his spiritual existence, lying like a dark lake in the midst. How, between mystery and mystery his mind, his wonder, his very reason, seem to rock like a little boat between the sea and sky. But speedily does he regain his serenity; when he throws himself, with childlike haste and confidence, into the arms of that Fatherly Spirit, and murmurs in his bosom, "How precious also are thy thoughts unto *me*, O God; how great is the sum of them"; and looking up at last in his face, cries—"Search me, O Lord. I cannot search thee; I cannot search myself; I am overwhelmed by those dreadful depths; but search me as thou only canst; see if there be any wicked way in me and lead me in the way everlasting." (Quoted in Charles Spurgeon, *Treasury of David*, Vol. 3, Part 2, p. 267.)

David begins his song (verses 1-6), recognizing that God's passion for him is *honest*. From the beginning, David decides in his mind that God not only truly knows, but He also knows "true-ly." God has perfect knowledge of us. This psalm reveals admiration, for whether it be man's actions, plans, speech, or even his thoughts, the king says, "O Lord, You know it altogether!"

Note the word pictures: the path and the pallet, the thoughts and the tongue, the encompassing (remember the last chapter?) and the empowering. In contrast to Proverbs 25:3 where Solomon writes, "As the heavens for height and the earth for depth, so the heart of kings is unsearchable," David confesses that compared to God's, his wisdom is nothing. God's omniscience is too wonderful (astounding) and high (beyond our comprehension). As Spurgeon wrote, " . . . when we stand a-tip-toe we cannot reach to the lowest step of the throne of the Eternal."

Filthy Rags

God truly knows. He really does know! His omniscience is as great as His omnipresence! His intimacy with us is just as great as His immensity. In Psalm 8:4, David is overwhelmed: "What is man that You are mindful of him, and the son of man that You visit him?" God is genuinely interested in us.

Furthermore, God knows "true-ly." He knows us as we really are. He fully comprehends and is never deceived, is never confused or indecisive in His ways. When we try to con Him by boasting of our worth, He simply reminds us that all our righteousness is like filthy rags. We bring to His attention our achievements, and He brings to our attention what He has done.

God Walks on Earth

As he was walking on the moon, James Irwin was overcome

with the thought that he was experiencing the greatest achievement in history. Think about it: "Man Walks on the Moon." About that time, God spoke to his heart and said, "No, the greatest achievement of all time was when God walked on earth!"

When I am aware that God passionately loves me and is infinitely interested in my situation, I can allow Him to control my life . . . even when it seems He is taking a sabbatical.

Carole and I often joke about the fact that we have three sons: Scott, born in California; Mark, born in Canada; and Derek, "made" in Hong Kong. From the time he could talk, Derek wanted a dog. Because at that time we lived in an apartment building with several hundred people surrounding us, we assured him there wasn't enough room for a dog. We did, however, promise that should we ever return to the United States, we would think about it. Of course, we never thought we would leave Hong Kong.

The Box of "Candy"

In June 1985 we made that drastic move. Eighteen months later, as we approached Derek's 16th birthday, we asked him what he wanted for this very special moment in his life. Of course, most boys whose psychological elevators reach the top floors of their brains would want either a truck, a car, or a girlfriend (usually in that order). But guess what the Hong Kong kid wanted? Yep, a dog!

I tried to explain that we were still living in a condo,

that we may have made a rash promise, or that we had simply lied! This discussion ended without a favorable resolution.

In January 1987, just six weeks before Derek's birthday, we were invited to speak for a Missions Conference in Portland, Oregon. While there, we stayed with some special friends. They owned a black and white shih tzu. You know, that's the Chinese dog with so much hair that you don't know which is the front or back until . . . it eats! Carole and I immediately fell in love with the shih tzu.

One morning I mentioned, "If I could find a dog like that, I'd get it for Derek's 16th birthday." The hostess replied, "It so happens that our dog has a sister whose master is moving. They are unable to keep the dog. If you would be willing to pay for its flight to Los Angeles, I'm sure they would be willing to give her to you. The dog's name is Candy."

That night they brought Candy for us to see. It was love at first sight! Arrangements were made to send the pet by air freight three days before our son's birthday. When Derek asked us about what we were getting him for his birthday, we simply responded, "A box of candy!"

I must tell you that our son is a basketball fanatic. When I told him we were going to the airport to pick up a special shipment, he asked me to get my staff to do it because the L.A. Lakers were playing the Chicago Bulls that night. "Fatherly Privilege" (or do they call it "Rule") prevailed and, against his wishes, Derek accompanied me to the airport.

The evening of destiny arrived, and Mother Nature treated Southern California to one of its hardest rainstorms in history. Furthermore, the important basketball game that was being simulcast over radio was not going according to Derek's liking. All the way to the airport, this 16-year-old adolescent complained, muttered "smart" comments, and made a pain of himself. When we arrived at the airport, we learned that the plane from Portland would be delayed for an hour or so. This did not help his mood one bit. Actually, while Derek snorted like a pig in the car, I went into the freight terminal.

The plane finally arrived, and Derek was summoned to come pick up the shipment. As he walked to the counter with the kennel and dog in full view, I exclaimed, "Congratulations, Derek! Here's your dog."

Looking right at it, he turned and said, "Dad, this is not the time to be joking. This is not a good night, nor is your humor appreciated!"

"Derek, that is your dog. I'm not joking. It truly is!"

"Does Mom know about this?"

"Son, remember the box of candy? There's the box, and your dog's name is Candy. Now go ahead and greet her!"

Just as he did, Candy licked his nose. He literally ripped the front off the kennel and grabbed the dog with excitement. I signed the bill of lading and left the staff of the freight terminal laughing at my delirious son.

Derek was already in the car, bouncing up and down in the back seat, yelling, "Wow, this is the greatest thing in the world. This is the best night of my life. Dad, you don't have to get me my driver's license." I almost jumped up and down! Of course, three days later he broke that part of the bargain!

Another Lesson

On the way home, I watched my son hug his "Candy." I was amused with the surprise we pulled on him. Then the Lord spoke.

"Ron, do you see Derek's delight? Remember his distress just an hour or so ago?"

"Yes, Lord, what are You saying? I've got a feeling I'm about to get nailed with a life lesson."

"How often, Ron, have you asked Me for your heart's desire? But when My answer did not come according to your plan, perspective, or expectation, you began to complain, doubt My ability, and even accuse Me of not caring. But then, when the answer did arrive, you forgot about all the accusations and exclaimed My wonder! Remember, Ron, that plane tonight left Portland long before you left for the airport."

How many times have we forgotten that God never forgets? When it seems that He has not heard or has chosen to ignore our plea, it simply means we are still "on our way to the airport." For He truly cares.

God passionately wants to bless us, even more than we can begin to imagine. He moves heaven and earth on our behalf, and even His divine delays are but temporary and protective. He is not satisfied with giving us any less than His best. And He'd rather die than have us miss His satisfaction. How do I know? Because He did die for us . . . on the Cross!

Study Questions
Chapter 6 ▪ Created With a Passion

1. How do emotions contribute to a sense of fulfillment and satisfaction?

2. Do most Christians truly believe that "God loves them
   unconditionally"?

3. How does knowing that God is omniscient shape your
   communication with Him?

4. Relate a personal experience where you doubted God,
   but later discovered that He was active all the time.

5. What does it mean to pray "according to God's will"?

His
Inescapable
Presence

Where can I go from Your Spirit? . . . Indeed, the darkness shall not hide from You, but the night shines as the day; the darkness and the light are both alike to You (Psalm 139:7, 12).

Whereas the first six verses of Psalm 139 speak of God's genuine passion for us, the next "stanza" (vv. 7-12) of that "song" informs us that His presence is inescapable. No matter where we go, God's Spirit and ours are interwoven and inseparable. There appear to be three interlinked aspects: God's passion for us, God's presence with us, and God's power to deliver and bring light to us, even in the dark seasons.

No Place to Run

David rehearses the omnipresence of the Almighty. Whether in the loftiest heights or lowest imaginable depths, God is there. God is even present at the edges of man's boundaries—the breaking of the dawn or the farthest depths of the sea.

Hidden in these words is a precious promise we dare not overlook. As David pondered the idea that there was nowhere to run, he talked about ascending into heaven and descending into Sheol (the grave or abyss). The same words were used by Zophar the Naamathite when he counseled Job:

> Can you search out the deep things of God? Can you find out the limits of the Almighty? They are higher than heaven—what can you do? Deeper than Sheol—what can you know? (Job 11:7, 8).

In Zophar's thinking, the phrase "higher than heaven" dealt with impossibilities. "Deeper than Sheol" referred to things beyond comprehension—mysterious things.

This thought also appears in Deuteronomy 30:11-14 (written at a later period than the Book of Job). God's conditions outlined here were subject to considerable reflection by Jews while in Palestine and after they were scattered by the Babylonians and Assyrians. (In his secular writings, Philo uses this text four times.)

> For this commandment which I command you today is not too mysterious for you, nor is it far off. It is not in heaven, that you should say, "Who will ascend into heaven for us and bring it to us, that we may hear it and do it?" Nor is it beyond

the sea, that you should say, "Who will go over the sea for us and bring it to us, that we may hear it and do it?" But the word is very near you, in your mouth and in your heart, that you may do it (Deuteronomy 30:11-14).

In Romans 10:6-10, the apostle Paul borrows from this Jewish passage when he answers the claim that Israel has not been given sufficient availability to the gospel:

But the righteousness of faith speaks in this way, "Do not say in your heart, 'Who will ascend into heaven?'" (that is, to bring Christ down from above) or, "'Who will descend into the abyss?'" (that is, to bring Christ up from the dead). But what does it say? "The word is near you, in your mouth and in your heart" (that is, the word of faith which we preach): that if you confess with your mouth the Lord Jesus and believe in your heart that God has raised Him from the dead, you will be saved. For with the heart one believes unto righteousness, and with the mouth confession is made unto salvation.

Because Jesus came to earth, putting a "face" on God, and because He rose from the dead, completing the perfect sacrifice for sin, the gospel is near and it is clear. Faith in Him is as close and as simple as one's mouth and heart.

He Is There

Coming back to David's usage of this same concept in

Psalm 139:7-9, we are comforted with the knowledge that God is not only passionately in love with us, but He is also present, capable of communicating with us. In 1 Corinthians 12:2, 3, we read that God is not a dumb idol unable to communicate with those who serve Him. Moreover, He has gifted His church so that at the very point of need, men and women can discover Jesus to be Lord. He assures us that wherever we are, He is there. Moreover, His intervention in our affairs will not bring confusion, but clarity. There is no better messenger than He who is the ultimate Communicator. And when we hear His message, hope returns, anxieties vanish, and we find satisfaction in the fact that God is with us.

In studying the life of Joseph we discover that during the most difficult times of his life, "the Lord was with him and . . . made all he did to prosper" (Genesis 39:3; see also vv. 21-23). The word *prosper* means "to prevail." The Lord's presence outlasted the predicament. At the end of Jacob's life, Joseph reflected on his own life. Standing before his brothers he concluded, "God sent me before you to preserve . . . your lives" (Genesis 45:7). Satisfaction comes when we realize that whatever our present circumstance, God's goal is to give us life . . . more abundantly.

God's presence brings with it His power. According to the psalmist, there is no difference between the darkness and the light with God. Not only should this be a concern to those who try to disobey in secret, but it is also a comfort to those going through difficult times. His power strengthens us to conquer any challenge.

Captured

"Please pray for my son, Shant," was one of the most

unusual prayer requests Dr. Harold Helms, senior pastor of Angelus Temple in Los Angeles, California, ever received. It was January 16, 1991—the day Operation Desert Storm broke out in the Middle East. Janet Harris was confident her son, Shant, was serving in the Iraqi armed forces. Her request was specific: "Pray that he will be captured by the United Nations Coalition Forces."

Janet immigrated to the United States in 1978, following a divorce in Baghdad. She brought with her two sons, the oldest was Shant Kenderian. The family settled in Chicago, Illinois, where Janet remarried and Shant continued his studies, earning exceptionally high marks throughout his first two years in high school.

In Baghdad, the Kenderian family were Armenian Christians. Shant's earliest memories included the message of Jesus. He was baptized in the Armenian Orthodox Church as a child. At the age of 6, he saw a brief vision of Jesus that made his faith a reality.

On September 14, 1980, Shant returned to Iraq to visit his father in Baghdad. One week later the war broke out between Iraq and Iran, and the borders were closed. Over the next eight years more than one million Iranians and a half million Iraqis lost their lives. To make matters worse, Shant's grandfather passed away in 1981, his father died in an automobile accident in 1982, and on January 6, 1984, his grandmother went to be with the Lord.

Through all the turmoil, Shant completed high school and earned a B.S. in production engineering in 1985. Shant and several other students held regular Bible studies. (One of his companions later entered the ministry.)

At this point in his life, Shant had a second vision. He was walking through a large house with someone he perceived to be his best friend. Their walk continued through many gates, narrow entrances into other rooms, and a hallway filled with reflections from a great light. As they walked, the light grew stronger, but the number of people in the vision lessened. With the number of available rooms and choices, they could have lost their way. However, because of the wise guidance of his friend, the right decision was made in each case. At the end of the journey, the friend revealed Himself to be the Lord Jesus. Little did Shant realize just how reassuring this vision would be to him in the difficult days that followed.

Upon graduation from college, Shant Kenderian was drafted into the Iraqi navy. For the next two and a half years the military base was bombarded by Iranian artillery. Living conditions were disastrous. Yet during that time, not one person in the unit was killed. Shant continued to study the Bible. Though Christianity was not the major religion of the country, Shant did not receive any opposition or persecution.

The war ended in 1988, and Shant was discharged in 1989. Deep in his heart the young veteran knew he must leave Iraq. Through correspondence he learned his mother and stepfather had moved to Glendale, California. When the borders of Iraq were reopened in January 1990, Shant was among the thousands who rushed to the American Embassy to reprocess their expired permits for entry into the United States. Lines were extremely long; the process painfully slow.

The Persian Gulf War

Time and hope seemed to run out on August 2, 1990,

when Iraq invaded Kuwait. The television and radio stations announced that all eligible men would be drafted into the armed forces. In a matter of hours, Shant Kenderian was again serving in Iraq's navy.

World tension grew during the next few months, and the January 15, 1991, deadline was set by the Coalition Forces. During this time, both Shant in Iraq and his mother in California felt a strong urge to pray. On the day the Coalition Forces began the liberation of Kuwait, Janet approached Pastor Helms.

Meanwhile, Shant was assigned to a landing boat as a mechanic. Sensing that his destiny was about to change, he volunteered for service on the front lines in the Persian Gulf armada. On January 24, 1991, at 11:30 a.m., his landing craft was on its way to the island of Qaru to evacuate personnel back to the naval base.

Shant had just completed a two-hour watch at the front of the vessel when the craft hit a floating Iraqi mine containing 600 pounds of TNT. His replacement, along with two others, was killed when the front of the vessel literally disappeared. Miraculously, there was no explosion even though a 36-ton fuel tank was burning! The remainder of the crew was rescued and taken to the island. Several hours later, they set sail for their home base.

Suddenly, their boat was attacked by a U.S. fighter plane. A bomb hit the rear of the vessel. The fighter was immediately followed by three helicopter gunships. Understanding that the gunner in the lead helicopter was demanding that the vessel be evacuated, the Iraqi crew obeyed. They boarded their life rafts and were picked up later by the frigate USS *Curts*.

Over the next few weeks, Shant was processed through

several POW camps. In each of the interrogations, he tried to convince the authorities that he had no immediate family in Iraq, but that his family was in the United States. Actually, though, because of his command of the English language they thought he was a spy. Miraculously, one of the guards assigned to Shant had been his schoolmate back in Chicago.

While in the camps, Shant was presented with the Word of God by his captors and chaplains. He participated in Bible studies with Coalition officers and enlisted men. Their mutual faith transcended the war. In the United States, his mother learned of his captivity. With the help of her pastor, she contacted the embassies and the American Red Cross.

One morning Shant was aroused from a sound sleep. The military policeman commanded, "Get your things together. You're leaving early in the morning for the United States." On April 15, 1991, he arrived in Los Angeles.

More Than Conquerors

I interviewed Shant extensively about lessons he had learned throughout this ordeal. He said, "If we keep our eyes and faith focused on God, we need not worry about the rest—our hope rests in the presence and power of God."

As for his mother, she said, "If we pray, God will answer. He is the only source of hope and safety."

Maybe the apostle Paul said it best:

Who shall separate us from the love of Christ?

Shall tribulation, or distress, or persecution, or famine, or nakedness, or peril, or sword? . . . Yet in all these things we are more than conquerors through Him who loved us. For I am persuaded that neither death [persecution] nor life, nor angels nor principalities nor powers [forces of evil in the universe], nor things present nor things to come [dealing with the course of time], nor height nor depth [fate or luck], nor any other created thing [the entire universe], shall be able to separate us from the love of God which is in Christ Jesus our Lord (Romans 8:35, 37-39).

God's Commitment

In His last discourse before going to the cross, our Lord promised He would not leave us orphans, but that He would give us another Comforter—Helper—who would abide with us forever! There is no period at the end of this promise!

A close connection exists between the omnipresence of God and His eternalness. While we are concerned about the immediate, His actions and decisions are made from the perspective of the everlasting. We are bound by the moment, but His knowledge has no bounds. We worry about what we are becoming today; He works according to what we shall be when we are made in His image! Our personal perceptions are short-sighted, unsure, and selfish; His are broad, long, and loving.

On my office desk in Hong Kong was a mat that said, "There is nothing that is going to come into my life today that the Lord and I cannot handle together. He is with me, and of that I am satisfied." God will complete all the conditions of His commitment to us.

Study Questions
Chapter 7 · His Inescapable Presence

1. How do God's passion for us, His presence with us, and His power in us interlink?

2. Has your "theology" become too complicated? How do you once again simplify it?

3. What is the Holy Spirit's role in communicating the gospel to the unbeliever?

4. How are the gifts of the Holy Spirit related to evangelism?

5. From the experience of Shant Kendarian, list three important applications for your life.

A
Great Work
of Art

For You formed my inward parts; You covered
me in my mother's womb. . . . I am fearfully and
wonderfully made. . . . I was . . . skillfully
wrought [made].

. . . The days [were] fashioned for me, when as
yet there were none of them.

. . . How precious also are Your thoughts to
me, O God! . . . (Psalm 139:13-17).

Carole and I are intrigued with Chinese arts and
crafts—paintings of Chinese children, cork
carvings, and embroidered pictures. Over the
fireplace we have vases covered with Chinese
calligraphy, jade artifacts, and cloisonné flower holders.
Because most of these are gifts from our Chinese friends,

they serve as reminders of love and the unique culture in which we ministered for more than 16 years. Their beauty is also now being shared with those who are hosted by the Williams family.

The Master Craftsman

When David considered the passion God had for him, He was amazed that God desired to have a relationship with him in spite of the fact that He knew him. David was overwhelmed that God would chase after him in every circumstance. How could this be?

In the third "stanza" (vv. 13-18) of this "song," we find the answer. He who feels greatest about his masterpiece will be the master craftsman. Simply stated, God is passionate about us because He made us.

"You formed my inward parts; You covered me in my mother's womb." The next time you dry off after a bath, admire the various parts of your body. Don't laugh. Just do it! The very fact that you can decide to follow my suggestion reveals a mind so intricately detailed that men and women spend their lives probing its possibilities. The ability to manipulate that towel requires the amazing teamwork of bone, muscle, and balance. The fact that you can even see where to put your towel involves the translating and arranging of impulses of light into patterns—a process that confounds the greatest thinkers.

Like David, we stand in awe at the intricacy of what we are. We become acutely aware that our life is totally dependent on forces other than our own. Rather than trying to act as the Creator (seeing ourselves at the center of everything), we return to our sense of being the created (seeing the value the Master Craftsman designed us to become). Rather than being degrading, such knowledge becomes delivering. You see, it is not what we own that brings a sense of belonging, but a knowledge of who owns us! And for the first time in our lives, we can be satisfied in simply being ourselves, the way God made us.

The Picture

When David talked about his being "covered" (v. 13) in his mother's womb, the Holy Spirit directed him to use a term translated today as "woven." This reminds me of a special "cat" picture in our front room.

On one of my trips to China, I visited Suzhou (Soochow). What a fascinating city! Established several millennia ago, the city is often referred to as the "Venice of the Orient" because it is built on a series of canals. I have stood on a bridge built by those who accompanied Marco Polo and tried to identify with men and women who for centuries walked the same path. What a mind-boggling experience. It was in this city that the vast majority of Chinese artisans and philosophers worked or learned their art.

While there, I was privileged to visit one of the factories which produces "weavings in silk." How fascinating to see young men and women at tables put "loops" (magnifying glasses) to their eyes, pick up one cat hair with a pair of tweezers, pierce it through a piece of stretched silk, and with a quick turn of the wrist, weave it right into the silk. This sequence is repeated over and over for 20 minutes, followed by a ten-minute rest for the eyes. When the work is completed, months later, the same picture appears on both sides of the silk. The silk is then pressed between glass and set in a rosewood frame. The cost of such a picture is certainly beyond my budget.

Several years later a friend purchased one of those pictures to express his love to us. Because no two pictures are alike, hardly a day goes by that we do not stop to admire the workmanship and expertise of this intricate work of art.

One of a Kind

These masterpieces are nothing compared to the care and personal attention that went into weaving our physical frames while we were in our mothers' wombs. Because He is the Creator, there is not a moment when God does not look down from heaven to admire His workmanship. He owns us, and we are His possession.

"I am fearfully [revered and respected, set apart] and wonderfully [distinguished, one of its kind] made" (v. 14). We belong to the Creator, and He has given us great worth—a value shared by no other. Recognizing that our value is set by Him rather than our peers frees us from comparison, competition, and contention.

The Vases

Before the earthquakes in Southern California on January 17, 1993, there was a ceramic vase setting in front of our fireplace. On it was the Chinese dragon (not demonic, but a symbol of man) chasing the pearl of success. The vase stood about four feet tall and was one of only two of its kind in the world. Unfortunately, it was broken in the earthquake. Now the only one of its kind in the world is located somewhere in the Orient. Later while visiting Hong Kong we discovered that the vase had been worth several thousand dollars. Again, we were reminded that our source of joy comes from who owns us, not from what we own!

In our kitchen is a gray ceramic pot marked: "Made in China." My wife uses it for mixing and baking. It has little outward beauty, but is very functional.

In their original forms, which of these two ceramic pieces had the greater worth? Both were equally valuable because each fulfilled its created function. One brought satisfaction to the eyes; the other tantalized our taste buds.

Made in His Image

As David discovered, our worth is determined by the glory of God and His purpose or function for us. Actually, that is the way I like to explain the term, the *Glory of God*. We were made in His image—His glory—with His purpose in us. We "fall short of the glory of God" (Romans 3:23) by not reaching the aim for which we were created. According to Colossians 1:27, Christ in us becomes our "hope of glory," or may I suggest a paraphrase, our possibility of fulfilling those purposes for which we were originally made.

I cannot begin to tell you what such a realization does to one's self-esteem. We do not have to compete with others to receive God's favor or to have self-satisfaction. Whether we are broke or bountiful, whether we are famous or forgotten, whether we have a high position or a humble responsibility, if we are doing God's will each day, we are always successful and full of God's glory. It is His estimate, not others' evaluations, that gives us worth!

"My frame was not hidden from You . . . [but] skillfully wrought." Wrought—embroidered! Not only do we belong to God, not only has He given us worth, but we can also look at ourselves as being competent. We are not just His possession for His pleasure, but we are made to play a significant part in His plan.

Oh, yes, Carole and I also have embroidered pictures hanging in our hallway. One is a silk embroidery of a hundred birds flying, sitting on branches and on the ground, and doing all sorts of things, with the sunrise in the background. It is called, "A Hundred Birds Greet the Sun!" I have counted everyone of those fowls—one hundred, exactly.

I asked the significance of the embroidery and its title. In the Chinese culture, the term *one hundred* signifies "all, total, complete, everyone." Birds represent people, and the sun often refers to deity. I suddenly interpreted the embroidery in our house: "All the nations greet the return of God himself."

Have you ever considered your significance in God's history? We know Noah, Abraham, Moses, David, the prophets, Mary, Elizabeth, Peter, Paul, Lydia, and others were placed in their particular times in history for unique reasons. Personally, because I have given much study to the letters of Paul, I plan to spend my first day in heaven looking him up and asking about some of his revelation. (Of course I won't need it then!)

I have heard others say they were going to find Isaiah to ask about his vision of the forthcoming assault of the Assyrians. Others want to ask Jeremiah about some of the wild things he did in prophesying judgment upon the nation. Still others want to interview the apostles about their days with Jesus on earth.

Redemption of Grace

But have you read 1 Peter 1 very closely? Listen to what he says . . .

> Of this salvation the prophets have inquired and searched carefully, who prophesied of the grace that would come to you, searching what, or what manner of time, the Spirit of Christ who was in them was indicating when He testified beforehand the sufferings of Christ and the glories that would follow. To them it was revealed that, not to themselves, but to us they were ministering the things which now have been reported to you through those who have preached the gospel to you by the Holy Spirit sent from heaven—things which angels desire to look into (1 Peter 1:10-12).

According to the patriarch of Pentecost, we will inquire of the saints of old, but they will also seek us out to ask how their prophetic words were fulfilled in the last days! Even the angels desire to learn more about the redemption of grace we enjoy, which they can only observe.

Consider this for a moment! In the same way that God placed all those people on the earth at strategic times to fulfill prophetic roles in redemptive history, He has counted us necessary to take vital roles in these last days. We have been placed on planet Earth at this moment to proclaim, like John the Baptist, the coming of the Lord. We are, as those birds, preparing to "greet the Son." Having a part in His plan is all we need to be satisfied.

"The days [were] fashioned [molded, formed, carved out] for me. . . . How precious . . . are Your thoughts to me." In using the term *fashioned*, David probably had in mind the woodwork in the king's palace, the hewing out of a hiding place in the rocks, and even the whittling of arrows and spears for battle. Not only was he the Lord's possession and pleasure, placed in the Lord's perfect timing for a special work, but his days were also carved out with a divine purpose in mind. Though I am sure that many of David's difficult days were caused by his own frailty, God turned those experiences into a process, King David's becoming—not just being declared to be—a man after God's own heart.

Working With Precious Stones

Remember my trip to Suzhou (Soochow)? My friend and I were invited to the studio of one of the most famous sculptors in China. There we saw a huge piece of jade worth hundreds of thousands of dollars that stood about six feet tall, four to five feet wide, and of equal depth. The veins of grey and white color running throughout the green surface were exquisite. The sculptor had carved chunks, large and small, out of the jade. He seemed to be totally without a plan.

I asked him what he was making. "A man," he replied. "In a few months, it will be placed in the national museum in Beijing." When asked about his plans, he pointed to his head and reminded me that he was a master craftsman. (By the way, from reports, he did meet his deadline.)

With my reasonably fluent Cantonese and horrible Mandarin, I expressed shock: "I don't understand why you seem to be so unorganized. If it were me, I'd start in one section, finish it completely, and then proceed to the next after the first part was perfect."

With a gleam in his eye, he smiled and responded, "I recognize two things: your Mandarin needs a lot of work, and you have no idea how to work with precious stones. If I followed your suggestion—perfecting one section before proceeding to the next—I'd ruin my work. You see, this stone is precious because it is still one piece. The stone could not withstand spending too much time carving on the same part. It would break, rendering the entire stone worthless. Thus, I work a bit here, take a lot out over there, and keep the angles balanced in my work. The work proceeds according to the texture of the jade. Remember, I'm a master craftsman. When I'm finished, it will be more valuable than it was in its original form. And, it will be a man."

The Ultimate Master Craftsman

Returning to the hotel, I felt embarrassed by my rudeness and obvious stupidity. Then, I received another life lesson from the Lord.

"Ron, isn't that the way I work with your life? I never

perfect one aspect of your life before going to another. If I did, you couldn't stand the pressure. You'd break! That is not my plan or my purpose.

"You see, you are even more valuable than any piece of jade. Therefore, this week I work on your worry, anger, and self-esteem. Next week, I deal with stewardship, pride, and love. The third week, I might return to some of those things already mentioned, or I might strengthen your faith. There are times I simply shave away small pieces of the old life. Other times, I dig deep, at the expense of causing you pain, and remove big chunks.

"But Ron, when I'm through with you and you enter the gates of My city, you'll look like a man. Remember, I'm the ultimate Master Craftsman. As a matter of fact, my son, You'll look just like me!"

> And we also glory in tribulations [pressure], knowing that tribulation produces perseverance [patient endurance]; and perseverance, character [constancy and consistency]; and character, hope. . . . For whom He foreknew, He also predestined to be conformed [molded or carved] to the image of His Son, that He might be the firstborn among many brethren. . . . In all these things, we are more than conquerors through Him who loved us (Romans 5:3-4; 8:29, 37).

Do you know that the greatest work of art in your home does not hang on the wall, but around the refrigerator? And that your most valuable possession does not grace your mantle, but your spirit? See yourself as God has made and is remaking you . . . and be satisfied with the progress!

There is nothing that will happen to you today—even though God might not cause it—that He cannot turn around to accomplish the following in your life:

- Personal growth
- The extension of His Kingdom's rule in others you touch
- The upbuilding of His Church!

Hallelujah, He truly is the Ultimate Craftsman!

Study Questions
Chapter 8 • A Great Work of Art

1. What "memorials" of God's goodness do you have in your home?

2. How important is it for you to have a sense of belonging? Explain.

3. How do comparison and competition hinder your sense of worth and satisfaction?

4. Identify your five strongest traits and tell how you bless others through them.

5. How do you normally seek the affirmation of others? What do you expect from them that will bring satisfaction and a sense of competence?

Part II

Our
Development

*As for me, I will see Your face
in righteousness;
I shall be satisfied when I
awake in Your likeness.*

–Psalm 17:15

A
Repentant
Heart

Create in me a clean heart, O God, and renew a steadfast spirit within me. Do not cast me away from Your presence, and do not take Your Holy Spirit from me. . . . The sacrifices of God are a broken spirit, a broken and a contrite heart—these, O God, You will not despise (Psalm 51:10, 11, 17).

The earlier chapters of this book describe God's role in bringing about life's highest delight—satisfaction in Christ. What elements in our lives contribute to our living out this satisfaction in our daily walk? The first element has to do with our hearts.

The Brightest Gem

The prayer of repentance in Psalm 51 is the most intimate and expressive of all of David's music. According to Victorinus Strigelius (1524-1569):

> This Psalm is the brightest gem in the whole book, and contains instruction so large, and doctrine so precious, that the tongue of angels could not do justice to the full development (Quoted in Charles Spurgeon, *The Treasury of David*, Vol. 1, p. 408).

In the eloquence of this artful gem, we are viewing the weakest moment in the king's life. The heart of the issue is one every man faces—the drive within that makes him the creator and head of the home, the achiever and leader God designed him to be. While we cannot overlook or despise this internal drive, we dare not take it for granted as did David. Sin, in this area, practically destroyed him. In fact, it did destroy his home, bringing him much grief.

Psalm 51 cannot be separated from 2 Samuel 11 and 12. In chronicling that account, the historian draws several contrasts.

The Temptation

We first notice David himself. Look how quickly this situation arose. The author notes that this was a time "When kings go out to battle . . . but David remained at Jerusalem" (11:1). When temptation came, David was not where he was supposed to be. Had he been involved in the battle, he would not have become preoccupied with the beauty of the wife of one of his soldiers.

Remember that the events of 2 Samuel 11 and 12 occur immediately after one of the strongest times in David's reign. The Ark of the Covenant had been returned to Jerusalem, and there was a period of peace and justice for the people of God. The Ammonites were defeated, but in one quick moment everything changed.

The Pattern of Sin

Follow the progression his sin took. He was intrigued by Bathsheba's beauty. It is not a coincidence that the channel of his attraction was through the eyes. Sounds like Eve's turmoil in the Garden of Eden: "And when the woman saw that the tree was good . . . that it was pleasant to the eyes . . ." (Genesis 3:6).

Intrigue turned to investigation. "A tree desirable to make one wise" was the way Eve described it in Genesis 3:6. To be attracted was not sin, but the decision to explore further was a choice of the will. Once investigation was initiated, involvement followed. Then "she took of its fruit and ate. She also gave to her husband with her, and he ate."

Likewise, David's act of sin did not end after the night with Bathsheba. Entrapment is always the result of sin's enticement and entrance. Calloused by his actions, David found a way of escape and excuse. The pattern has not changed:

> Blessed is the man who endures temptation; for
> when he has been approved, he will receive the

crown of life which the Lord has promised to those who love Him. Let no one say when he is tempted, "I am tempted by God"; for God cannot be tempted by evil, nor does He Himself tempt anyone. But each one is tempted when he is drawn away by his own desires and enticed. Then, when desire has conceived, it gives birth to sin; and sin, when it is full-grown, brings forth death (James 1:12-15).

Uriah

In contrast, let us look at Uriah. In Scripture, Uriah is listed as one of the 37 mighty men closest to David. By command and personal choice, he had a strong commitment to the king. His loyal obedience was startling when compared with the king's disobedience before God.

Uriah maintained a strong loyalty to his men—those who fought the front lines. Refusing self-gratification, even an earned night of rightful pleasure with his wife, this mighty man chose the doorstep of the king's house as his place of rest. Not for one night, but two! Uriah's self-control made David's self-indulgence even more conspicuous.

Still, Uriah became the victim of another's sin. He was sent back into battle to be sacrificed to the hands of the enemy. Really, there were two enemies; we all know which one was the worse.

Joab

Enter Joab. This entire event was imprinted with the

complicity of Joab. Because of his loyalty, Joab became an accomplice to murder. By not even questioning the orders of the king in light of God's standard, he became part of the cover-up. Sin was almost made to sound acceptable.

With today's marvelous teaching about the grace of God, some people fear that by setting standards they are guilty of legalism. Thus, the church often becomes as guilty as Joab by not asking, "Isn't there a difference between God's ways and the ways of sin?"

Legalism is defined as "relying on our own obedience to the works of the Law as the basis for justification." First of all, we are incapable of keeping the way of the Lord perfectly. Of course, if we could, it would not be necessary to be declared righteous through Christ.

Holiness, on the other hand, is not simply a *separation* from the defilement of sin's rule in our lives, but it is the *selection* of the more excellent way of having the Spirit rule in our hearts. Holiness is a positive walk that leads to perfection, setting a standard higher than that of the Law. May we remember that the Biblical standard for believers is a choice between better and best, rather than between what is right or wrong. To expect a life of excellence from those who belong to God, who is the Most Excellent One, is not legalism. It is legitimate and life-changing.

Nathan

Unlike Joab, the prophet Nathan confronted David with a parable. This was not only divine, but it was also dangerous.

According to the laws by which David governed the nation, both adultery and murder required the death penalty. So did slander of the king. Had David's heart not been convicted, Nathan would have been condemned to death for treason. But in light of God's Word—not in spite of such consequences—the man of God stood before the king. Could this prophet be a type of the Holy Spirit in His role in dealing with sin in our lives?

The Trap

Recently I learned how the Eskimos in Alaska catch wolves that attack their herds. A sacrifice from the herd is made, knives are dipped in its blood and stuck into the frozen ground with the blade exposed to the elements. After repeating this several times, the blood forms "Popsicles" on the blades of the multiple knives encircling the field or herd.

The wolves are then overcome by their lust. As they lick and then suck the bloody knives, their desire increases until they no longer seek the animals themselves, but lust after the taste of the blood. Even after the sacrificed animal's blood totally disappears from the knives, the wolves continue to lick and suck. By this time, however, they are eating their own tongues and licking their own blood.

No Satisfaction

If we do not deal with sin at its onset, its attraction will increase until it destroys us. Unconfessed sin in our lives is not only dangerous but it is also disastrous. Consequently, as long as sin remains, there will be little satisfaction.

As soon as David recognized his sin, his heart was broken before the Lord. According to Psalm 51, repentance broke forth with remorse and the recognition that God was completely just in dealing with and allowing the consequences of the king's sins. Although she is not mentioned further in the context of this particular event, Bathsheba's guilt and grief were no doubt just as great as David's.

Unfortunately, even when the sentence of death for his sin was removed through God's forgiveness, the scars remained. A few days following their firstborn's birth, the child of David and Bathsheba died, just as Nathan prophesied. The child was never even given a name.

Proper Relationship

Fortunately, when the sentence of sin was removed through God's forgiveness, the relationship was restored. Later, as David comforted Bathsheba, she conceived and bore him a son, Solomon, also called Jedidiah, "Beloved of the Lord."

What caused David to repent? It was not because he had been caught; rather, it was something about the character and person of God that drew the king back into proper relationship. These thoughts are listed in Psalm 51.

God is merciful (Psalm 51:1, 2). David realized that God was willing to forgive him; He was, as it were, "waiting in the wings" for his return. *Mercy, lovingkindness, tender mercies, blot out, wash, cleanse* are all words that invite us to come to Him.

There is a difference between God's having mercy and God's excusing sin. In recent years, the term *justification* has been explained by the cliché, "Just as if we had never sinned," and has perhaps been represented by the bumper sticker, "I'm not perfect, just forgiven." But God never blindly overlooks our state of unrighteousness or our unrighteous acts. Forgiveness is ours, based solely on His mercy. He forgives us because He wants to, in spite of our guiltiness and unworthiness.

Look at Israel. Even after Israel rejected Jehovah's teachings and the Messiah himself, the Scripture says, "All day long I have stretched out My hands to a disobedient and contrary people" (Romans 10:21, which quotes Isaiah 65:2). It sounds like His arms are still open, reaching for us!

God is fair (Psalm 51:3, 4). David declared, "That You may be found just when You speak, and blameless when You judge." Mercy flowed from the heart of God in dealing with David and Bathsheba's sin.

The apostle Paul wrote the words in Romans 3:4 in reference to the excuses of humankind. Sinful men and women claim God is unfair in punishing their unrighteousness. David, like Paul, said God will be true and just, even if every man is a liar.

David said in Psalm 51:3, 4 that if God were tried in court for His handling of the sin, God would be declared totally fair and innocent. His acts were just and were properly administered according to the reality of the sin. When we approach God with repentant hearts, we know He will deal with us in the same manner.

God is trustworthy (Psalm 51:5, 6). David recognized that true righteousness did not originate in the things done, but in who he was. He confessed his battle with his inner flesh.

Like David, we must acknowledge the same problem. Unlike him, however, we most often do not confront it. We would rather do spiritual warfare with the demons of Satan that enslave those in far-off lands, than to fight the battle with our carnal nature and its satanic demands.

In our terms, truth always deals with the past in light of the future. God is able to deal with the inner man, maintaining equilibrium in the repentant heart. Two things are kept in balance: the expectation of God and the pro-vision of God.

When we place our trust in God, He brings worth into our lives. He becomes the stabilizing factor, bringing fresh perspective, a proper sense of value, and satisfaction.

God is forgiving (Psalm 51:7-9). These verses refer to the ceremony for becoming clean, outlined in Numbers 19. The declaration of cleanliness by the priest declared the positional implication of a restored relationship with a just and pure God. Not only are our sins forgiven, they are also forgotten!

In David's day, washing did not imply the use of an electric machine, but rather a process of pounding and beating the garment. Impurities were forced out, and the cloth was dried by the light and heat of the sun until it met the expectation of the owner. In the same way, true forgiveness does not permit us to be passive, but encour-ages us to offer restitution to those wronged as we turn from the impurity itself. This cleanliness comes only by instruction and correction of the Lord.

God is present (Psalm 51:10, 11). In David's own words, the presence of the Lord was essential to him. He begged for the Holy Spirit not to be taken from him. A clean heart must be created by God; steadfastness will be a process of continuing renewal.

As we approach the Lord with a repentant heart, it is His desire to birth new life in us. In Romans 5:3-5, we not only rejoice in the pronouncement of our favored position in Christ, but we also boast (rejoice) in the process in which we ourselves become what we already are in Him. That process includes pressure (tribulation) which brings forth perseverance (patience). In turn, patience (constancy or consistency) develops character. The final outcome is hope which will never make us ashamed, because the love of God has been poured out in our hearts by the Holy Spirit, who has been given to us.

When God allows pressure, tension, or suffering to come into our lives, it is to birth new hope within us, never to destroy the hope we already possess. In Romans 8, the term *groanings* is used three times. Paul states that "creation groans" (v. 22), "we . . . groan" (v. 23), and the Holy Spirit groans (v. 26). *Groanings* in this passage refers to "birth pangs," not "death throes." As our hearts remain humble, our present sufferings bring forth prevailing hope, new maturity, and areas of personal dominion over sin, and ultimately we are conformed to the image of God's Son.

God is redemptive (Psalm 51:12, 13). God restores us, is generous to us, and then uses us to teach others. This will result in the conversion of other sinners. Through our experiences we are empowered to help others who face the same challenges. Please note the connection with satisfaction: "Restore to me the joy of Your salvation, and uphold me by Your generous [good] Spirit" (v. 12).

Looking back at the time of struggle mentioned in the Introduction, I now realize that I was experiencing a terrible onslaught of the devil. I experienced depression that just would not go away, and permitted that negative spirit to rule my attitude, my home, and my office. That spirit robbed me of joy in my ministry by permeating every conversation and clouding every relationship.

Restored by the grace of God, I began to talk about my experience. From this experience I have been able to counsel many, many people going through the same thing. Seeing that many identified with my struggle led me to write this book.

I would never be so presumptuous as to say that God caused my struggle. Nor do I want to give any credit to the devil by saying, "He made me do it." There is no one to blame except myself. But I declare with confidence that what had been instigated by my own carnality has now been turned into help for others because of the Savior's forbearance, forgiveness, and foreknowledge. God will take whatever is occurring in your life and turn it from bondage into blessing, both in your own life and in those of others around you.

God is pleased with a contrite heart and a broken spirit (Psalm 51:14-19). David announced that true sacrifices could not be found in busyness or performance. True sacrifice is the attitude of the heart. Freedom results from a humble and grateful spirit. Worship results from a humble and grateful spirit. Boldness in witness results from a humble and grateful spirit. Service and ministry result from a humble and grateful spirit. Success and maturity result from a humble and grateful spirit. Let us therefore approach God with humble and grateful spirits.

It was while he was under house arrest in Rome that Paul came in contact with Onesimus. In keeping with his lifestyle and purpose, the apostle led the young man to the Lord. Then he discipled him.

One day during their conversation, Paul happened to ask where the lad lived. The boy's reply was, "Colossae, just a few miles from Ephesus."

"Oh, yeah," said Paul, "I have a great friend there. As a matter of fact, he was saved in one of my meetings in Ephesus. He and his brother-in-law are pastoring a congregation in Colossae. His name is Philemon."

Onesimus' face turned red as he confessed, "I know Philemon. The reason I'm here is that I just robbed him blind!" The young man continued, "I wish I could return to him and be reconciled."

The result of this encounter was Paul's letter to Philemon, found in the New Testament, which says in brief: "Receive Onesimus, because he is now what his name implies—profitable."

The Joy of the Lord

David repented and became a man after God's own heart. He dared to approach a God who is merciful, fair, trustworthy, forgiving, present, redemptive, and who delights in the heart that is humble and grateful before Him.

There can be no satisfaction in my heart unless there is repentance. If there is sin that is unforgiven or if I hold unforgiveness toward others, I will not experience the joy of the Lord—that which gives me strength. I will continue to be a slave to the very person I have not forgiven.

Even as this topic is included at the very center of this book, repentance is the heart of the matter for everyone who seeks the satisfaction of God.

Study Questions
Chapter 9 ▪ A Repentant Heart

1. Define repentance and remorse. Compare the two.

2. Contrast the steps of David's failure with the trials in your own experiences. List the lessons to be applied.

3. Do you agree with the author's definition of "legalism"? What is the relationship between God's grace and the believer's personal responsibility?

4. Are there times when God seems unfair? How can you overcome the feelings of guilt for issues that are already forgiven?

5. Does forgiving others contribute to personal satisfaction? Explain.

Chapter 10

A Spirit-Controlled Walk

Restore to me the joy of Your salvation, and uphold me by Your generous [liberating] Spirit (Psalm 51:12).

Therefore do not be unwise, but understand what the will of the Lord is. And do not be drunk with wine, in which is dissipation; but be filled with the Spirit, speaking to one another in psalms and hymns and spiritual songs, singing and making melody in your heart to the Lord (Ephesians 5:17-19).

David inserted a very vital request while composing his Song of Repentance. He connected the restoration of joy (satisfaction) with God's liberating Spirit. Centuries later, the apostle Paul suggested that making melody in our hearts is a direct result of being filled with the Spirit. In other words, *turning away* from sin and its consequences must be followed by a *turning toward* righteousness and its freedom.

David pleaded that he be upheld by God's *generous* Spirit. Actually, a better translation of the term would be "liberating." It is equivalent in Paul's writings to 2 Corinthians 3:17: "Now the Lord is the Spirit; and where the Spirit of the Lord is, there is liberty." This word is found again in Galatians 5:1: "Stand fast therefore in the liberty by which Christ has made us free" (see also v. 13). In Ephesians 5:18, we are instructed not to be drunk or satiated (the same root word as satisfied) with wine which brings chaos and destruction, but we are admonished to be filled with the Holy Spirit who brings order and fulfillment. Liberty, satisfaction, and submission to the control of the Holy Spirit are intricately linked.

For most of my Christian life and ministry I did not understand the concept of being "filled with the [Holy] Spirit" (v. 18). This phrase carried with it a mystifying sense of passivity in which the supernatural guidance of the Holy Spirit was anything but "super-practical." Then came one of the greatest challenges of my ministry.

Doing God's Work

By 1973, the Williams family had ministered in Hong Kong almost four years. I tackled the challenging assignment with gusto, dedicating major chunks of time to the work. Unfortunately, I neglected the most important assignment—my family. Although my wife tried to warn me, I excused myself with the presumption that if I did God's work, He would take care of my sons. My error was in the very real truth that I was *not* doing God's will.

Yes, doing God's work without doing His will is possible!

One morning I overheard our oldest son, Scott, age 9, tell his mother he had "lost his daddy to Jesus." His words shocked me! Over the next several months, not only did I give more attention to the family, but I also began a search in the Scriptures to find the Biblical principles that should govern the priorities between the ministry and the home. A powerful passage dealing with these priorities is Ephesians 5 and 6.

Walking in the Spirit

Until that time, I always separated Ephesians 5:15-21 from the rest of the passage. As I examined the text, it dawned on me that these verses were talking about walking wisely and understanding the will of the Lord, with the Holy Spirit as the center of my life. Moreover, the apostle painted a picture for us of a Spirit-filled and Spirit-led person.

A husband led by the Holy Spirit submits to and loves his wife as Christ loved the church (5:25-29). A wife led by the Holy Spirit submits to and receives life from her husband in the same way the church relates to Christ (5:22-24; 33). Spirit-filled parents model the Christian life and train their children in the same manner (6:4). Spirit-filled children honor and obey the leadership of their parents (6:1-3).

This principle even impacts the workplace. Those who are doing the will of God serve their masters (employers or supervisors) with sincere respect, as if the Lord were their boss (6:5-8). Those who do the will of God from the heart treat their employees with respect as pleases the Lord in heaven (6:9).

God's Priority

Above all, those who redeem the time (take full advantage of it) recognize that their battle is not with flesh and blood. A Spirit-filled Christian will put on the armor of God for protection, and use the weapons of God so that His purposes may be accomplished (6:10-20).

I believe these relationships mentioned in Ephesians are listed according to God's priority. We cannot be a spiritual person unless we have a proper relationship with the Holy Spirit of God. We cannot effectively love our mates unless our own spiritual lives are in order. There is no successful parenting without successful homemaking. If we do not experience a good home or marriage, there is no way we can be effective in our work or vocation. Service performed for God will have credibility only if the other areas of our lives are under the Spirit's control. This principle is as true for ministers and missionaries as it is for church members! I have written often, "What does it profit missionaries, if they gain the whole world, but lose their own children!" In his excellent book, *In Step With the Spirit*, Rubel Shelley suggests it is our reliance on the Holy Spirit to be *president* of our lives, not simply a resident, that makes the difference:

> The terminology used by Paul in Galatians, chapter 5 is most significant. He turns from acts of the flesh to fruit of the Spirit. Acts are something one can do by acting on their own

impulses; fruit is a passive element that happens as a result of something done inwardly. The flesh acts; the Spirit bears fruit. Therefore, fruitfulness in the power of the Spirit of God is grace-based, not works-based (p. 22).

For some Christians, the excitement of Christianity has turned into routine and monotony. The reason is that they have not yet understood that the new life we live in Christ is more on being than doing. Being God's yielded vessel in whom the Spirit of God can really live to bear fruit is what matters, not doing all the things we have come up with in our self-help manuals as crucial for proving we are genuine Christians in the strength of the flesh (p. 13).

Developing Christian Character

One of my favorite movies is *Driving Miss Daisy*. In the film, the chauffeur receives constant instructions from Miss Daisy on where to go and how to get there. Knowing better, the driver simply replies, "Yes, Miss Daisy," and, with tender care and attention, takes the best roads. Upon arrival at their destination, Miss Daisy sometimes recognizes his wisdom.

May I dare suggest that this is a picture of our Christian lives? We sit in the back seat demanding this and that of God, while He continues developing our Christian character through better roads (experiences), better care (lessons and teachings), and greater attention (provision and protection). Could it be that being led by the Holy Spirit is simply the choice to sit in the "back seat" and leave the driving to Him? Could it be that being filled with the Spirit is yielding to God's priorities and principles in every situation that comes our way?

In his letter to the church in Galatia, Paul moves us from "what" to "how." He writes, "Walk in the Spirit" (Galatians 5:16 and 25). There is no competition or comparison. To walk in the Spirit is simply to follow His footsteps.

Before going to Hong Kong as missionaries, Carole and I pioneered a church near Vancouver, British Columbia. Although the people and scenery were marvelous, there were two difficult winters with heavy snowfalls. Pioneering this church also meant hours of shoveling long driveways. The short path from our porch to the driveway was bordered on both sides by shallow ditches. When it snowed these were hidden. Because I knew exactly where the ditches were, I first "stepped out" a path to the car and then called the family to follow my size 12 footprints. Thus, they were able to walk to the car without falling off the path (most of the time)!

Our two sons were 5½ years and 18 months old, respectively. They could not have followed if I had taken adult strides. The length between my steps had to be adjusted for them. If we had stayed longer in Canada, the space between the steps could have lengthened as they grew.

Each day, as we follow in the footsteps of the Holy Spirit through the Word, listening to His still small whisper in prayer, and learning lessons from our experiences, our *spiritual steps* are being lengthened. For new believers, the steps are short. But as we grow stronger, our stride is stretched, demanding greater faith and effort. The goal is to walk as spiritual adults, not according to our own determination and effort, but by His direction and enablement.

The Fruit of the Spirit

As we follow Him in obedience, we develop these qualities in our character:

- We will be more loving.
- We will experience greater joy.
- We will respond more peacefully.
- We will serve others with greater patience.
- We will be kinder.
- We will develop a spirit of goodness and loyalty.
- We will have a gentle spirit.
- We will exhibit stronger self-control.

These characteristics are listed in Galatians 5:22, 23 as the fruit of the Spirit.

The term *fruit* is better translated as "produce, product, or harvest." This harvest is produced by the Spirit's leading and our obedience to that leading, and pertains to character, rather than charisma. Walking in the Spirit is a continual process; it is not a gift we are given.

Have we ever asked God for more love only to see Him put someone in our lives who was unlovely? How many times have we prayed for patience and then discovered stronger opposition? Then there are those times when we desired greater self-discipline, only to be confronted by the temptation to remain unchanged. Could it be that God is more interested in our reactions than our actions? Who we are is far more important to the Lord than what we try to do in our own strength.

I have discovered that the fruit listed in Galatians is only a partial list. Romans 12:9-21 describes how the fruit of the Spirit gives credibility to the gifts of the Spirit (vv. 3-8). In 1 Corinthians 13 we read how love is lived out according to the harvest of the Spirit. This same thought is continued in Ephesians 4:1-6, Colossians 3:5-17, and Philippians 4:1-9. Qualifications for leadership in the church are found in 1 and 2 Timothy and Titus. Out of 20 qualifications listed in Timothy and Titus, only one has to do with ability. The others are exemplary of mature character.

When we comprehend that the Christian life is not striving to achieve these qualities, we are relieved of the pressure to perform. Failure on our part is not the end of our relationship with God; it is part of the learning process. No longer are we compelled to reach a list of two dozen goals for living the Christian life, but only ONE—following in the Spirit's footsteps in each decision and discipline. When we are totally obedient, we see the results of the harvest.

Spiritual Growth

Carole and I now live in sunny Southern California. One morning, I decided to plant some flowers on our front veranda. Because of past failures, my wife laughed when I told her my plan. I almost decided to rename her Isaac (remember Sarah?).

While purchasing the bulbs, the salesperson told me to see that the soil was nurtured with light and water. I returned home, planted the bulbs, and checked on the progress of the plants each morning.

Although I watered the soil every day, I saw no signs

of growth. It was tempting to dig up the bulbs and see what was taking place. My better judgment assured me that doing so would kill any progress, so I decided to patiently follow the instructions and keep watering. Weeks later I was rewarded with sprouts, then stems, and finally a whole flower pot of blooms. I permitted my wife to keep her original name while we both enjoyed the beauty of my flowers.

What was the key to my success as a botanist? Patiently maintaining the soil with light and water. In time the blooms burst forth.

As we continue to water our hearts with God's Word and the light of God's Spirit, we too will see the blooms of spiritual growth and maturity. A Spirit-controlled walk is not only attainable, it is life's highest delight!

Study Questions

Chapter 10 ▪ A Spirit-Controlled Walk

1. From Ephesians 5 and 6, diagram the six arenas of life in which "being filled with the Spirit" will be modeled.

2. Compare your present priorities with those outlined in Ephesians 5 and 6.

3. Respond to the statement by Shelley: "Fruitfulness in the power of the spirit of God is grace-based, not works-based."

4. What is the difference between "being filled with the Spirit" and being baptized in the Holy Spirit?

5. In living out the "fruit of the Holy Spirit," what responsibility does the believer fulfill?

An
Attitude
of
Joy

You have put gladness in my heart. . . . The righteous shall be glad in the Lord, and trust in Him. And all the upright in heart shall glory. . . .

But let the righteous be glad; let them rejoice before God; yes, let them rejoice exceedingly. . . .

Let all those who seek You rejoice and be glad in You; and let those who love Your salvation say continually, "Let God be magnified!" (Psalm 4:7; 64:10; 68:3; 70:4).

E vidence of our satisfaction is joy—the state of a glad attitude. The word *evidence* is used because of the many promises and statements of joy and gladness in the believer's pattern of living. In these days of unusual pressure, stress, and change, joy can easily become lost in the Christian's life.

The Joy of the Lord

Joy is an internal quickening that creates contentment (satisfaction) and emotional well-being (gladness). The source of joy is the Holy Spirit. Unlike the world's view of happiness, joy is not bound up or conditioned by what goes on about us. Joy is not determined by our circumstances, but triumphs in the midst of them, creating in us strength and the confidence that life is really worth living.

The Scripture states, "The joy of the Lord is your strength" (Nehemiah 8:10). The development of a glad or joyful spirit imparts to us a portion of God's character that braces us for victory in every situation.

Yes, joy is part of the character of God. Look at the atmosphere of God's presence:

> Oh, clap your hands, all you peoples! Shout to God with the voice of triumph! . . . God has gone up (been victorious) with a shout, the Lord with the sound of a trumpet. Sing praises to God, sing praises! . . . For God is the King of all the earth; sing praises with understanding (Psalm 47:1, 5-7).

> Great is the Lord, and greatly to be praised in the city of our God, in His holy mountain. Beautiful in elevation, the joy of the whole earth, is Mount Zion . . . the city of the great King . . . (Psalm 48:1, 2).

His creation is full of rejoicing:

> Say among the nations, "The Lord reigns. . . . Let the heavens rejoice, and let the earth be glad;

128

let the sea roar, and all its fullness; let the field
be joyful, and all that is in it. Then all the trees
of the woods will rejoice before the Lord (Psalm
96:10, 11, 12).

There was joy in its creation:

Where were you when I laid the foundations
of the earth? . . . When the morning stars
sang together, and all the sons of God shouted
for joy? (Job 38:4, 7).

We picture heaven as a place of serenity and quietness.
But the more I learn of God and His surroundings—
thunderings, lightnings, singing, rejoicing—the more I
picture heaven as a place of voluminous sound, a holy
cacophony of rejoicing!

The major acts of God were accompanied with joy.
On that first Christmas Eve, the angels sang tidings "of
great joy" which were to be to all people (Luke 2:10).
The writer to the Hebrews reminds us that "for the joy
that was set before Him" our Lord endured the cross
(12:2). At His resurrection, the women who saw the risen
Lord were filled with joy (Matthew 28:8, 9) and ran to
inform the disciples. Those same disciples returned to
Jerusalem "with great joy" (Luke 24:52) following the
ascension of Jesus.

At the Messiah's return,

The ransomed of the Lord shall return, and come
to Zion with singing, with everlasting joy on their
heads. They shall obtain joy and gladness, and
sorrow and sighing shall flee away (Isaiah 35:10).

God will wipe away every tear from their eyes (Revelation 21:4). Then he will announce:

Well done, good and faithful servant. . . . Enter
into the joy of your lord" (Matthew 25:23).

We have not yet begun to exhaust the scriptures that
refer to the presence of joy and gladness being part of the
person and work of God. A proper theology of God cannot be developed without including in it a theology of joy
and gladness.

It is God's desire that His sons and daughters be people
of joy. With the promise of the Messiah came the fore-
cast of joy:

> The Spirit of the Lord God is upon Me, because
> the Lord has anointed Me to preach good tidings
> to the poor; He has sent Me to heal the
> brokenhearted . . . to console those who mourn
> in Zion, to give them beauty for ashes, the oil of
> joy for mourning, the garment of praise for the
> spirit of heaviness; that they may be called trees
> of righteousness, the planting of the Lord, that
> He may be glorified (Isaiah 61:1, 3).

Thus, ". . . with joy you will draw water from the wells
of salvation" (Isaiah 12:3).

After talking to His disciples about abiding in Him,
the Vine, Jesus told them He spoke these things that His
joy might remain in them and that their joy might be full
(John 15:11). He prayed that the disciples would have
His joy in their lives (see John 17:13).

Harvesting Joy

This provision of joy was also intended for the early
church. The gospel was received in Samaria with "great
joy" (Acts 8:8); the letters from the Jerusalem Council

130

caused the new Gentile believers to be glad (Acts 13:48). Writing to the believers in Rome, Paul told them, "Let your hope make you glad" (12:12, *CEV*); "The kingdom of God is . . . righteousness and peace and joy in the Holy Spirit" (14:17). He prayed that the God of hope would fill them with "all joy and peace in believing" (15:13). He then asked them to pray for him that he might come to them, following his trip to Jerusalem, "with joy by the will of God" (15:32).

To possess a Biblical lifestyle we must develop this life view of joy:

1. *Joy and gladness in our lives will be in direct proportion to whether or not we allow the Holy Spirit to mold our character.* Joy is listed as one of the manifestations of the fruit of the Spirit (Galatians 5:22, 23). These are called *fruit* because they are the result—the product or harvest of being led by the Holy Spirit rather than being something we attain to or obtain in some other way. Take another look at the previous chapter in this book.

2. *Joy and gladness will be in direct proportion to our willingness to forgive.* Repenting of his sin with Bathsheba, David asked that the joy of his salvation be restored (Psalm 51:12). Such joy came from the king's yielding to the Lord and receiving His instruction. "Therefore," David says, "my heart is glad, and my glory rejoices. . . . You will show me the path of life; in Your presence is fullness of joy" (Psalm 16:9, 11). If you lack joy in your life, check your "Forgiveness Chart," with God and with man. Only as you live in light of God's forgiveness will joy be available. And only as you learn to forgive others, without expecting any return, will you experience joy.

3. *Joy and gladness will be in direct proportion to our devotional life.* Jeremiah testified, "Your word was to me

the joy and rejoicing of my heart" (15:16). Jesus promised us, "Until now you have asked nothing in My name. Ask, and you will receive, that your joy may be full [complete]" (John 16:24). Without exception those times in my life when I am without joy are when I neglect my daily discipline of spending time in prayer and reading God's Word.

4. *Joy and gladness will be in direct proportion to our sacrifice in serving others.* Those who sow in tears will be the ones who reap with songs of joy (Psalm 126:5). Often we don't reap joy because we fail to sow in tears. In this world of instant gratification, we fail to experience the satisfaction that results from sacrifice. In the end, we are the losers!

Our joy and gladness will be either hindered or enhanced by our overall attitude. Christ desires that we focus on Him in our daily routines. He works in us to will and to do His good pleasure. But frequently we become more focused on things about us than on His purpose. We need to cultivate the attitude that "His anger is but for a moment, his favor is for life; weeping may endure for a night, but joy [literally, a shout of joy] comes in the morning" (Psalm 30:5, 6).

Enjoying the Present

For many years the Foursquare Gospel Church in Macao operated a Children's Home. As many as 60 children between the ages of 4 and 19 were housed, fed, clothed, and educated because of the love of ladies across North America who sponsored these children. Today many of these children are pastors of churches and leaders in their communities.

Not only did the Children's Home take in orphans, but it provided care for children who had been abandoned or whose parents could not properly care for them. One such child was 8-year-old Lee Yin Kuen. This lad, the youngest of 12 children, was born to a family who lived on a fishing boat in the Macao harbor. Because of Lee's uncontrollable demeanor and their own frustration, his parents tried on several occasions to drown him.

Because A-Kuen was pudgy—just like someone else I knew at that age—he and I became good friends. It was my responsibility to supervise the operation of the Home, so I made monthly trips for business and inspection. Each Christmas we were able to purchase gifts, coats, shirts, skirts, underwear, socks, and shoes for everyone with special donations. You can imagine the reaction when I ordered 57 dozen pairs of socks and underwear. When asked how many children I had, my answer always overwhelmed the salesperson. I would end up having to see the manager!

The day after Christmas each year, the Williams family traveled by jet-foil to the Children's Home to attend a service, distribute gifts, and accompany the children to a special Chinese celebration feast. Joy filled the entire occasion. These are some of our greatest missionary memories.

For me, however, Christmas 1980 was to be different. I had just handled some very difficult situations in our churches in Hong Kong. My father had also passed away earlier in the year. On the way to Macao, I turned to my wife and said, "I'll just have to endure the celebration this year." The word miserable wouldn't begin to describe my feelings that day.

Approaching the Children's Home, we were met by Lee Yin Kuen. He couldn't wait to tell me that he was going to get a new pair of "ball shoes" for Christmas. "What color?" we asked. He grinned from ear to ear and giggled, "Brown." The celebration began, the clothes were passed out (including A-Kuen's brown ball shoes), and we boarded a double-decker bus to take us to a special barbecue.

I sat in the back of the bus looking down the aisle toward the front doors. Sitting in the front of the bus was Lee Yin Kuen. As the bus made its way through the crowded city streets, the boy looked out the window to enjoy the scenery. Then smiling, he lifted his feet to look at his new shoes. Every two to three minutes, this was repeated.

Watching him from the back of the bus, I envied his joy. Forgetting the horrendous experiences of his past and the uncertainty of his future, this young boy enjoyed the thrill of the present. His focus was on the simplicity of the moment and the gift from a lady who dared to love one she had never seen. Here we were, Lee Yin Kuen with his simple, childlike joy, and Ron Williams with his complex, sophisticated frustration. My envy was followed by tears.

Rejoice in the Lord

While focusing on the circumstances around me, I had lost sight of the purposes of God. I forfeited the joy and gladness God wanted me to have at that moment.

Philippians 4:4 encourages us to "Rejoice in the Lord

always. Again I will say, rejoice!" A glad spirit comes by enjoying the now—God's gift of life that covers my past, assures my future, and gives grace for the present. His joy is always available in a quiet, still, inner strength. Joy gives us power to triumphantly transcend the turmoil with peace by faith. The result: Greater satisfaction with our God!

> It is good to give thanks to the Lord, and to sing praises to Your name, O Most High; to declare Your lovingkindness in the morning, and Your faithfulness every night, on an instrument of ten strings, on the lute, and on the harp, with harmonious sound. For You, Lord, have made me glad through Your work; I will triumph in the works of Your hands" (Psalm 92:1-4).

Study Questions

Chapter 11 • An Attitude of Joy

1. Define joy and explain how it becomes your strength.

2. What robs a person's joy? What usually robs your joy and why does it?

3. Do the Word and prayer have an appointment on our daily schedule?

4. Why does "unselfish giving" contribute to your joy?

5. Is "enjoying the now," a regular experience in your life? Why would Jesus emphasize this in His Sermon on the Mount (Matthew 6)?

A
Scripture-Fed
Mind

Your testimonies I have taken as a heritage forever, for they are the rejoicing of my heart. I have inclined [bent] my heart to perform Your statutes forever, to the very end (Psalm 119:111).

On a recent El Al flight to Israel, I sat across the aisle from two Hasidim. Observing the rituals of these devout Jewish gentlemen, I realized their depth of dedication in performing God's statutes.

Hasid is a Hebrew word meaning "devout" or "faithful." The Hasidic movement is a mystical form of Jewish culture instigated in the 18th century in Poland. At that time Polish nobility wore long, black coats, black knee britches, white stockings, and broad-brimmed hats, often trimmed with fur. The Hasidim adopted these fashions many still wear today. A local resident in Jerusalem told us that some of the fur hats could cost as much as $1,000 in U.S. currency. That's "putting your money where your head is!"

Hasidim maintain a very strict code of behavior in diet, dress, and daily prayer. The men follow the admonition of Leviticus 19:27 by not shaving their beards or sideburns. They meticulously roll their sideburns to keep them out of the way.

The Hasidic women dress modestly in clothes with long sleeves, high necks, and heavy stockings. Since it is forbidden for any man other than her husband to see her hair, she wears a head scarf or a wig.

Three thousand years ago God instructed His people, Israel, to observe a code of rules wherein foods must be clean or fit. To be kosher, food is prepared in certain ways, and only certain animals, fish, and birds may be eaten. The rules of kashruth (Jewish dietary laws) extend even to what foods may be combined with others. Dairy products are never to be eaten with meat or poultry. A kosher home always has separate dishes, separate dishtowels, sometimes even separate sinks, for dairy and for meat.

As the sun began rising across the eastern horizon, I watched the Hasidim don their prayer shawls, edged in elaborate embroidery, for the first of three times of prayer. I was fascinated as I watched them pull up the left sleeves of their shirts, and wrap their arms seven times with black leather strips (called tefilin or phylacteries). Many other Jews, devout though not Hasidim, observe this ritual.

Finally, the gentlemen pulled out what looked like tiny black boxes attached to leather straps. This they wrapped around their foreheads. Thus prepared, they began praying, right there in the aisle of the Boeing 747 at 40,000 feet. These religious men were obeying God's command to bind His Law "as a sign on your hand, and they shall be as frontlets between your eyes" (Deuteronomy 6:8).

Binding His Word

I am not suggesting that believers today adopt a new fashion style, diet (although some of us could use better rules of eating), or worship. I am suggesting that one reason many of us do not find the satisfaction God desires for us is that we haven't *bound* His Word around our hands or between our eyes. There is a direct relationship between God's Word and our satisfaction. Destiny and deliverance are not found in "boxes," but in the Bible! David wrote that when he bent (inclined) his heart to live according to God's principles and patterns, the testimony of the Lord brought rejoicing.

Inclining our heart is much more than legalistic obedience or adherence. Knowing God's written covenant determines our view of His person and His promises. Our foundation for belief is in His Word to us.

First, "binding" His Word is believing that what God has written in Holy Scripture is holy, set aside. The Word of God is His standard, not merely His suggestion. God is not simply offering us good advice, He is revealing His divine will. The bottom line is whether or not we believe God is serious about what He has written.

The Bible is the very foundation of our faith. His Word is not merely inspiring, it is inspired—God-breathed and God-begotten. We must receive the Word at face value and at "faith value." Psalm 119 teaches us . . .

- The Word cleanses our way (v. 9).

- His testimonies strengthen our soul (v. 28).

- His truth causes us to walk in salvation and liberty (v. 45).

- His statutes become our song (v. 54).

- His precepts revive us (v. 88).

- His commandments become as sweet as honey (v. 103).

- His promises hide us in hope (v. 114).

That is why the apostle Paul cautioned his spiritual son, Timothy:

> But you must continue in the things which you have learned and been assured of, knowing from whom you have learned them, and that from childhood you have known the Holy Scriptures, which are able to make you wise for salvation through faith which is in Christ Jesus. All Scripture is given by inspiration of God, and is profitable for doctrine, for reproof, for correction, for instruction in righteousness, that the man of God may be complete, thoroughly equipped for every good work (2 Timothy 3:14-17).

Paul's admonition to Timothy is the conclusion of a segment in which he deals with a number of problems: the unprofitable striving over words which brings ruin to hearers; youthful lusts which are quarrelsome rather than gentle and patient; and becoming enslaved to a powerless religiosity—ever learning but never turning to the knowledge of the truth. If we find a substitute for God's Word, we will never find the substance of God's satisfaction.

Second, "binding" His Word implies that what God has caused to be written is to be adopted as the sovereign authority in every situation. We do not adapt the Word to our circumstances. We adapt the circumstances to His Word. We must change, not God! David wrote, "Forever, O Lord, Your word is settled [stands firm] in heaven" (Psalm 119:89).

I have ministered extensively in several cultures. One of the statements I dread to hear is, "But I'm not sure it will work here." I believe in the wisdom of understanding culture and its context in applying the Scriptures; nevertheless, when social form contradicts Biblical principle, the Bible must always be accepted as the final authority. God's Word changes the circumstances, not adapts to them.

There is a difference between Biblical principle and personal preference (or dare I say, prejudice). When I first traveled to Asia, I was not accustomed to many of the cultural forms. I had to discern between what was God-originated (Christianity) and those practices or interpretations which were products of my own culture or tradition (Church-ianity). The two seemed so intertwined that they were hardly distinguishable to me.

I also believed everything had to have an explanation and that it was my task to come up with the answers. Then I learned and accepted the fact that revelation never has to be fully explained to be received. Furthermore, revelation should be explained only to the extent to which it is revealed. You and I get in trouble when we try to prove our point or defend a particular interest beyond what the Bible actually says. Should we lose the debate, often our joy and even our hope dissipates. Our sense of satisfaction is gone!

When it comes to the Word of God, there is never a question as to who is right. There is only One who wins any argument—God himself. Accepting the Word of God for what it says frees you and me from having to come up with answers to everything. On truths clearly stated in the Bible we stand firm; on all others, we wait for further understanding or for the day when we will be in full agreement—when we will know God as we are known by Him. The most satisfying and honest answer we have for some questions is "God knows; I don't."

A third aspect of binding God's Word to our hands and our heads is that God's Word is to be experienced, not merely exegeted. It is to result in living beyond explanation.

But haven't experts—Biblical critics—proven the Bible to be reliable, accurate, and authentic? Yes, and we should admire scholars for their discipline in patient research, examination, and evaluation. Because of their endeavors we can be certain that our Bible translations are correct and credible. However, the tendency most of us have is to try to examine and analyze the Bible, rather than simply to enjoy it.

Dr. Dick Scott, president of LIFE Bible College in San Dimas, California, recently addressed the opening convocation of a new semester. He likened the Word of God to a divine love letter. Taking the metaphor a step further, he said, "Suppose Ted writes a love letter to Sally. In it he writes, 'My Dearest Beloved, You are the apple of my eye. I desire to be with you and to look into your beautiful face. I want you to be happy and will do everything I can to see that you are. Will you marry me? Love, Ted.'"

The contextualist would question, "In what mood and

surrounding circumstance was Ted when he wrote the letter? Is there something else happening that we should know before we pass judgment on the letter?"

The textualist would ask, "Why did Ted choose the concept of the apple? Moreover, is there anything further that should have been added following the word *are* in the next to the last sentence?"

The philosopher would observe, "Is Ted's attraction to Sally based on her beauty or on his pity of her, seeing that she doesn't seem to be happy?"

The theologian would try to analyze the steps Ted takes, from seeing to desiring to committing. Finally, the theologian would examine the doctrine of whether or not Sally was "predestined" to marry Ted. Would her yes be of her own free will?

Or what if Sally never opens the letter, or perhaps reads only the first part? She may not even get the point of the marriage proposal!

This example has been overstated simply to suggest that all Ted really meant to say was that he loved Sally and wanted her to marry him! However, by the time the text is analyzed, the romance is drained from it. Sally is no longer sure if Ted wants to be her husband or her counselor, and Ted questions why he wrote the proposal in the first place. Maybe he should have asked her in person.

When was the last time you read the Word of God without trying to make it fit into some system of analysis? Aren't there some things in the plan of God that we are meant to simply enjoy and never fully understand?

Finally, binding God's Word to our foreheads and our forearms suggests that we know the Scriptures. Before I can

accept His Word as the standard to be adopted and enjoyed in every aspect of my life, I must know what God
has actually said.

Having taught hundreds of students and counseled dozens of adults during 30 years of ministry, I do not find the
greatest problem of Christians to be a lack of zeal or hunger for God. Instead, it is a lack of knowing what the
privileges and pleasures are that God has provided for
His children. Many are unaware that God has provided
everything necessary for life and godliness.

Enjoy Freely

The story is told of an immigrant family who saved
every dime to move to the new land of America. Because
of the cost of the tickets, the family had no extra money
to purchase food. All they could afford was peanuts, dry
bread, and water. While other passengers enjoyed the
ship's cuisine, the mother and father gathered the children into a corner in the lower deck to feed them their
daily rations.

The ocean liner docked at the pier in New York two
weeks later. Glad that their ordeal was over, the family
gathered their belongings to disembark. As they walked
down the gangplank the captain stopped them and inquired
where they had been for the past 14 days—why had they
not enjoyed the facilities of his ship.

The captain was aghast when he heard the father's explanation. "My good man," he responded, "didn't you
know when you bought the tickets that all the meals on
the ship were included? Didn't you read the brochure or
the back of your tickets that explained all the facilities

you could freely enjoy? All your family's meals were paid for in advance."

Too many of us, like the family in the story, do not enjoy our Christian experience simply because we have not read God's brochure of grace—His Word.

In my private study at home hangs a painting of an elderly Chinese gentleman. He is pictured stroking his straggly beard with one hand while the other hand holds the paper tablets of wisdom the old man is reading intently. I have written below the painting, "Your testimonies have I taken as a heritage forever, for they are the rejoicing of my heart."

Happy is the man who reads God's love letter and in simple faith believes that God means what He says and that His way really works! It really does!

Study Questions
Chapter 12 ▪ A Scripture-Fed Mind

1. Explain the difference between making God's Word the standard rather than a suggestion.

2. What function does the Word of God have in the development of your faith?

3. In your opinion, do most believers differentiate Biblical principles from their own religious preferences?

4. Is there a distinction between reading God's Word and studying it? What are the benefits of "Bible reading"?

5. Do you have a consistent, comprehensive plan of reading and memorizing the Word of God?

Chapter 13

A
Spirit
of
Worship

Oh come, let us sing to the Lord! Let us shout joyfully to the Rock of our salvation. . . . "Oh come, let us worship and bow down; let us kneel before the Lord our Maker. . . . Do not harden your hearts. . . . So I swore in My wrath, 'They shall not enter My rest'" (Psalm 95:1, 6, 8, 11).

This past Thanksgiving one of my sons asked if he could have the key to the storage bin in our garage. His two brothers accompanied him in a digging journey through those piles of boxes in an adventure that would challenge Indiana Jones. An hour later the three dusty "voyagers to the bottom of the abyss" returned with boxes filled with family photos that covered five generations of the Williams family. For the next four hours, the entire clan laughed—at times almost to tears—recalling different interpretations of past experiences. The grandkids were introduced to their fore-fathers, and we all made comments about how much everyone had grown and changed. I couldn't believe the different hairdos one of my sons had between the ages of 15 and 20!

We were completely exhausted, but exhilarated after having gone through those pictures and slides. We finally called it a night and promised to continue our trip down memory lane at Christmas. As I joined one son on the sofa, he looked at me and said, "You know, Pop, God has given us a marvelous life!" I shook my head in agreement. With tears in our eyes we thanked God for His providence in merging the past with the present. Together we worshiped . . . and were satisfied.

The *Rest* of Worship

Psalm 95 appears to be one of a series of songs the Israelites sang on their way to the Temple in Jerusalem, to celebrate and offer sacrifices to Jehovah. This is one of the most significant songs ever written by the shepherd-king outlining the majestic details of worship. The last half of the psalm is quoted in Hebrews 3 and 4 and warns believers about falling into the same trap that ensnared the children of Israel in the desert. Although the Israelites saw God at work throughout their journey in the wilderness, they did not learn what it meant to bow down and worship. Thus, they never entered into the rest (the Sabbath) God designed for them.

David begins the song by inviting God's people to sing, shout joyfully, and approach the presence of God with thanksgiving. Not only is God's worth declared (vv. 1, 2) but His work is also celebrated (vv. 3-5). Worshiping Him results in sharing God's life (vv. 6, 7) wherein He is set apart as our God, and we are set apart as the people of His pasture and the sheep of His hand. Finally, God begins to instruct us to find *menuchah*—"a place of rest, stillness, peace, and satisfaction." The Great Shepherd wants to lead us beside the waters of *menuchah* (Psalm 23).

The purpose of worship is not to feed God's ego or to console any loneliness He might feel by our lack of adoration. Worship is not limited to fulfilling our moral obligation to "glorify Him as God" or willfully be thankful (Romans 1:21). But Isaiah 6 declares that seeing the Lord in worship will . . .

- Quicken the conscience by God's holiness (vv. 1-4)
- Feed the mind with God's truth (v. 5)
- Purge the soul by God's fire (vv. 6, 7)
- Open the heart to experience God's love (v. 8)
- Devote the will to God's purpose (vv. 8-11).

Temptation

However, the children of Israel did not find the waters of *menuchah*, only the wilderness of *Massah* ("strife" or "tempting") and *Meribah* ("contention"). In Psalm 95:8-11, David referred to history recorded in Exodus 17:2-7 and in Numbers 20:7-13, when Israel put God's ways on trial and decided they had a better plan.

The Israelites were delivered from Egypt. They crossed the Red Sea on dry land and experienced God's miracles. They danced before Him, giving honor to Him for His triumphant victory. But when they came to Marah, their music suddenly turned to murmuring and complaining. God responded by making the bitter waters sweet. At Elim, God provided a second oasis where they could find rest. He then began a "food distribution program" to feed them in the desert until they reached the Land of Promise.

However, when the Israelites came to Rephidim they asked Moses, their leader, for water. God instructed Moses to use the same rod he had held when God parted the Red Sea, and told him to strike the rock. Water sprang forth and quenched the thirst of the people. The place was named Massah and Meribah, because it was there they tested God.

Nearly 40 years later, the Israelites revisited Meribah and again asked for water. They should have known better. Between the two visits the Law had been given, as well as rules for the sacrifices and for the setting up of the priesthood. There had been numerous victories, despite their lack of faith at Kadesh-barnea. It has been said, "Those who do not learn the lessons of history are usually bound to repeat them!"

There was another difference, however. Forty years older and wiser but very tired, Moses heard God's instruction to *speak* to the rock. Yet when Moses became angry, he reacted rather than resting in the Lord's promise, and hit the rock twice with the rod he had used on the previous visit. God provided the water, but because Moses disobeyed, he was not permitted to enter the Promised Land. And God was grieved.

What lessons can we learn about worship?

1. *Coming before God with a true spirit of worship will always exalt His worth, not ours.* An understanding

of His worth will change the manner in which we approach Him and will give us a sense of awe which will dissipate rebellious spirits and demands that His ways conform to our desires.

One of the sites which deeply impressed me on my visit to Israel was the Western Wall in Jerusalem, also known as the Wailing Wall. The only remaining relic of the last Temple, it is the holiest of all shrines to Jews.

The Western Wall is a portion of the retaining wall that Herod built around the second Temple in 20 B.C. In the year 70 A.D., just as Jesus foretold in Matthew 24, the Roman general Titus destroyed the Temple, leaving no stone unturned. This part of the wall was spared, its huge blocks being the only remaining trace to show future generations the magnitude of the Roman destruction of the great Temple.

During the Roman period, Jews were not allowed to enter the city of Jerusalem. During the Byzantine period, they came once a year on the anniversary of the destruction of the Temple, to weep over the dispersion of their people. From 1948-1967 they were not allowed to visit the wall because it stood in the Jordanian section of the city. Following the Six-Day War, the Wailing Wall became a place for national rejoicing and worship. Some believe it to be the present resting place of the Spirit of God upon Israel.

Because of the sacredness of the site, no Jewish person would think of turning his or her back to the wall while approaching or leaving the wall, especially during prayer. This would be a sign of disrespect for the holiness of God. This behavior, Jews feel, would represent an undue familiarity with God, bringing the Lord down to being only a peer with whom they could relate in colloquialisms and indiscriminate attitudes.

Hearing of the Jews' respect for the divine presence of Almighty God brought conviction to me. I am thankful that Jesus came to live on earth with man, but often I become too presumptious of His presence, relating to Him on my terms, rather than His. How often have I treated Him as my religious mascot rather than my Master? We must be sensitive to the fact that God is not our good buddy. He is our Creator—holy, righteous, and worthy.

The *"worth-ship"* of God is the foundation of our worship. When we fully respect His Person, we will not use cute or clever religious clichés or ever make light of Him. We will approach Him in humility, honor, and holiness. This will bring a balance between shouting for joy and bowing at His feet.

I am not advocating a return to forms of religiosity. Neither do we fear His sovereignty. We, instead, will worship Him with reverence, as we partake of His grace.

2. *Coming before God with a true spirit of worship will place demands on us, not on Him.* Charles Spurgeon wrote:

> Over the forty years, the Israelites put the Lord to needless tests, demanding new miracles, fresh interpositions, and renewed tokens of His presence. Do not we also peevishly require frequent signs of the Lord's love other than those which every hour supplies? Are we not prone to demand specialties, with the alternative secretly offered in our hearts, that if they do not come at our bidding we will disbelieve? . . . Friendship only flourishes in the atmosphere of confidence, suspicion is deadly to it: shall the Lord God,

true and immutable, be day after day suspected by His own people? (*The Treasury of David,* Vol. 2, p. 167.)

True worship will always result in true living. The forty years of Israel's contrariness actually nauseated God! Spurgeon continues:

> It is no small thing which can grieve our long-suffering God to the extent which the Hebrew words here indicate, and if we reflect a moment we shall see the abundant provocation given; for no one who values his veracity can endure to be suspected, mistrusted, and belied, when there is no ground for it, but on the contrary the most overwhelming reason for confidence . . . Which shall we wonder at, the cruel insolence of man, or the tender patience of the Lord?

Dangers

Over the past two decades, the church has experienced renewal in corporate worship. Praise and spontaneous worship are becoming widely accepted. This freshness in our celebration of the Lord brings restoration to the people of God. Contemporary forms of music and freedom of expression are bringing personal experience back into the realm of theology. While this has created some legitimate concerns in the more traditional segment, new life, for the most part, has come into our services and liturgies.

Along with the good, however, are some dangers. Many music lyrics emphasize what *we* get from God, rather than who *He* is and what *He* has done. Scriptures have even been taken out of Biblical context. In some cases, we have omitted the context of passages which call Israel to repent for spiritual adultery and have unwittingly turned them into victory marches in which we claim to triumph over the enemy. Often we have sacrificed truth for taste. As a result, we are shallow, immature and inefficient in waging spiritual battle. We have become proficient in planning worship hours, but desperately deficient in soulwinning. Moreover, we have made worship a substitute for other Biblical experiences in our congregations, such as Christian education, sanctification, and so forth.

Another danger is our perception of what true worship is. We spend much of our time and energy going through forms of worship—raising our hands, moving to the music, clapping our hands, and bowing before the Lord. By the time the sermon rolls around, we are so exhausted from standing that we have difficulty concentrating on the content of the message. We leave the morning service with bandages on our spiritual hurts rather than the spiritual surgery we need for our carnality. We have not been nurtured from the preached Word, yet we feel we have worshiped!

But, have we really worshiped? Or was what we experienced just a form of spiritual aerobics? While our corporate celebration should include wonderful physical expressions from our heart, unless our worship places greater demands on us than it does on God, we will not find the *menuchah*, or "satisfaction," which will sustain us during wilderness wanderings. At the same time that we are seekers who are sensitive in our forms of worship, we must maintain the attitude of seekers who are willing to be changed.

3. *Coming before God with a true spirit of worship should occur on weekdays, as well as on the weekends.* Worship has to do with life, not liturgy. While in the wilderness, the children of Israel kept the regulations Jehovah required of them. Yet Psalm 95:10 says, "It is a people who go astray in their hearts, and they do not know [in practice] My ways."

One of the most quoted verses in the Bible is Romans 12:1:

> I beseech you therefore, brethren, by the mercies of God, that you present your bodies a living sacrifice, holy, acceptable to God, which is your reasonable service.

Some expositors have legitimately translated the phrase "reasonable service" as "rational worship."

Presenting Our Bodies as Living Sacrifices

Our rational worship is the presenting of our bodies as living sacrifices. Paul was not inserting a new idea in his letter to the church at Rome. He was summing up what he had already written. In chapter 6 the verb "present" is also used in verse 13:

> And do not present your members as instruments of unrighteousness to sin, but present yourselves to God as being alive from the dead, and your members as instruments of righteousness to God.

Rational worship is presenting our bodies as channels through which daily, righteous living flows.

In 1 Samuel 15:22, Samuel confronted Saul's rebellion with these words:

> Has the Lord as great delight in burnt offerings
> and sacrifices, as in obeying the voice of the
> Lord? Behold, to obey is better than sacrifice,
> and to heed than the fat of rams.

Let us never forget that our life of worship extends throughout the week and is not just during the hour on Sunday when we corporately celebrate what God has done in our lives. There is no option! Both are necessary if we are to find *menuchah*—rest and satisfaction.

4. *Coming before God with a true spirit of worship benefits us more than it benefits God.* The messianic Psalm 22 contains an essential truth regarding worship:

> But You are holy, enthroned in the praises of
> Israel. Our fathers trusted in You; they trusted,
> and You delivered them. They cried to You, and
> were delivered; they trusted in You, and were
> not ashamed (vv. 3-5).

Commenting on this verse in *The Spirit Filled Life Bible,* Dr. Jack Hayford writes:

> Few principles are more essential to our
> understanding than this one: the presence of
> God's kingdom is directly related to the practice
> of God's praise. The verb "enthroned" indicates
> that wherever God's people exalt His name, He
> is ready to manifest His kingdom's power in
> the way most appropriate to the situation, as
> His rule is invited to invade our setting. . . .
>
> God awaits the prayerful and praise-filled
> worship of His people as an entry point for His
> kingdom to "come"—to enter, that His "will be
> done" in human circumstances. We do not
> manipulate God, but align ourselves with the

great kingdom truth: His is the power, ours is the privilege (and responsibility) to welcome Him into our world—our private, present world or the circumstances of our society" (Jack W. Hayford, Psalm 22:3 "Establishing" God's Throne, *The Spirit Filled Life Bible,* Thomas Nelson.)

God is not fickle! Nor is He insecure! While He enjoys and receives our worship, I believe His purpose is beyond our understanding. In His magnificent wisdom, God so designed worship that we can receive His supernatural power and relate His eternal presence to our lives today.

We should praise God that we do not have to make the same mistakes the children of Israel did in Psalm 95. We can have soft hearts that shout joyfully before the Lord rather than "trying" our Creator. We can proclaim His great works, rather than grieve Him with our pride. The result? We shall enter His *menuchah*!

Study Questions
Chapter 13 ▪ A Spirit of Worship

1. Trace the Biblical references on worship through the Psalms. Is there a difference between our traditional worship services and Biblical worship?

2. Why do you think God asks us to worship Him?

3. How does the practice of worship impact our attitudes and speech?

4. Why do believers at times take God for granted when they worship?

5. Is there a connection between worship and sanctification? How does worship become a lifestyle?

Chapter 14

The
Fruit of
Our
Lips

My heart is overflowing with a good theme; I recite my composition concerning the King; my tongue is the pen of a ready writer. . . . My mouth shall tell of Your righteousness and Your salvation all the day, for I do not know their limits. I will go in the strength of the Lord God; I will make mention of Your righteousness, of Yours only. . . . It is good to give thanks to the Lord, and to sing praises to Your name, O Most High; to declare your lovingkindness in the morning, and Your faithfulness every night. . . . For You, Lord, have made me glad through Your work; I will triumph in the works of Your hands (Psalms 45:1; 71:15, 16; 92:1, 2, 4).

Has your heart ever been stirred to the extent that you simply *had* to write about your experience? At such times, it seems that nothing can keep the words from coming. The expressions of the heart quickly flow across the page with exactness and excellence. In the psalmist's case, these were lyrics to be placed to another melody. Many feel they could have been a wedding song between the heavenly Bridegroom and His elect spouse. In any case, the beauty of the Lord and the blessing of His bride were announced with gladness (satisfaction) and rejoicing. The Lord gave David this song.

The Mouth Speaks

This chapter is not about divine composition, but about how the penmanship of our tongue can bring glory to God, salvation to our day, and gladness to the work of our hands. As the author of Proverbs states:

> A man will be satisfied with good by the fruit of his mouth, and the recompense of a man's hands will be rendered to him (Proverbs 12:14).

> A man shall eat well by the fruit of his mouth, but the soul of the unfaithful feeds on violence. He who guards his mouth preserves his life, but he who opens wide his lips shall have destruction (Proverbs 13:2, 3).

Jesus spoke about the relationship between our heart and our mouth:

> For out of the abundance of the heart the mouth speaks. A good man out of the good treasure of his heart brings forth good things, and an evil man out of the evil treasure brings forth evil things. But I say to you that for every idle [barren or unemployed] word men may speak, they will

give account of it in the day of judgment. For by your words you will be justified, and by your words you will be condemned (Matthew 12:34-37).

Here our Lord was speaking to the unbelieving religious leaders in His day who thought the miracles He was performing were not the work of God but of the devil. Because of the healing power of Jesus, a man who had been blind and mute now saw clearly and spoke with clarity.

Those religious leaders who claimed to be the visionaries and voices of truth were actually worse off than the healed man was in his original state. Their hearts could not see and their speech was *unemployed*—of no use at all.

From the good treasure and abundance in the heart, the mouth speaks forth that which builds faith to all who hear them. James talks about the power of the tongue:

> If anyone does not stumble in word, he is a perfect [complete and finished product] man, able also to bridle the whole body. . . . The tongue is a little member and boasts great things. See how great a forest a little fire kindles! . . . But no man can tame the tongue. It is an unruly evil, full of deadly poison. With it we bless our God and Father, and with it we curse men, who have been made in the similitude of God. . . . Who is wise and understanding among you? Let him show by good conduct that his works are done in the meekness of wisdom . . . the wisdom that is from above is first pure, then peaceable, gentle, willing to yield, full of mercy and good fruits, without

partiality and without hypocrisy (James 3:2, 5, 8, 9, 13, 17).

Taming the Tongue

God desires control of the most unruly member of our body, our tongue! It is His purpose to take that which defiles the whole body and make it pure. God wants to change tongues that ignite fires into tongues that kindle peace. When God controls our tongue, we are no longer stubborn as a horse which needs a bit in its mouth, but we become gentle, willing to yield.

The same tongue which once proclaimed messages of envy, pride, confusion, and profanity will now speak wisdom with credibility, pure words full of sincerity that bring forth a harvest of righteousness. Rather than a weapon of destruction, the tongue will now be a well of delight through which people will hear from God and be satisfied with Him.

The following blessings are a result of wholesome and wise speech:

> The mouth of the righteous is a *well of life*. . . . *Wisdom* is found on the lips of him who has understanding. . . . The tongue of the righteous is *choice silver.* . . . The lips of the righteous *feed many.* . . . The mouth of the righteous brings forth *wisdom.* . . . The lips of the righteous know what is *acceptable* (Proverbs 10:11, 13, 20, 21, 31, 32).

> The thoughts of the righteous are *right.* . . . The mouth of the upright will *deliver* them. . . . A [righteous] man will be *satisfied with good* by

the fruit of his mouth. . . . He who speaks truth *declares righteousness.* . . . The tongue of the wise promotes *health.* . . . The truthful lip shall *be established* forever. . . . Those who deal truthfully are *[the Lord's] delight* (Proverbs 12:5, 6, 14, 17, 18, 19, 22).

A man shall *eat well* by the fruit of his mouth. . . . He who guards his mouth *preserves his life.* . . . The lips of the wise *shall preserve* them. . . . A soft answer *turns away wrath.* . . . The tongue of the wise *uses knowledge rightly.* . . . A wholesome tongue is a *tree of life.* . . . The lips of the wise *disperse knowledge.* . . . A man *has joy* by the answer of his mouth, and a word spoken in due season, *how good it is!* . . . The words of the pure are *pleasant.* . . . A good report makes the bones *healthy* (Proverbs 13:2, 3; 14:3; 15:1, 2, 4, 7, 23, 26, 30).

Righteous lips are the *delight of kings.* . . . The heart of the wise teaches his mouth, and adds learning to his lips. Pleasant words are like a *honeycomb, sweetness to the soul and health to the bones.* . . . He who has knowledge spares his words, and a man of understanding is of a *calm spirit.* . . . The words of a man's mouth are *deep waters;* the wellspring of wisdom is a *flowing brook.* . . . A man's stomach shall *be satisfied* from the fruit of his mouth; from the produce of his lips he shall be filled (Proverbs 16:13, 23, 24; 17:27; 18:4, 20).

The lips of knowledge are a *precious jewel.* . . . He who loves purity of heart and has grace on his lips, *the King will be his friend.* . . . The sweetness of a man's friend *gives delight* by hearty counsel (Proverbs 20:15; 22:11; 27:9).

When we look closely at these verses, we discover every quality that Paul lists in Galatians 5 as the fruit of the Holy Spirit. These qualities will become part of our demeanor when we place Him as watchman of our mouths. Further examination reveals three distinguishing manifestations of the prophetic gifts of the Holy Spirit—edification, exhortation, and encouragement.

Satisfied With God

How do we recognize those who are satisfied with their Lord?

1. *They will not take the name of the Lord in vain.* I'm not referring to four-letter words as much as to the false prefacing of everything with the claim, "I have a word from the Lord," or "The Lord told me. . . ." One who speaks for the Lord never has to announce it. If his words are from the Lord, everyone else will know it. Saying "This is a word from God for you" is very convenient because it's hard to disagree with God.

2. *A satisfied Christian will talk more about eternal possessions than material possessions.* The wise man wrote, "The backslider [the one who is not progressing] in heart will be filled with his own ways, but a good man will be satisfied from above" (Proverbs 14:14). They will talk more of God's acceptance of them, than of their accomplishments for Him. In fact, when someone gives them praise, they might even be embarrassed.

3. *One who is satisfied with the Lord will be slow to*

hear rumors and be very selective in flattering others.
He will always be aware when someone else fails that
"There, but for the grace of God, go I." Such a one will
be more interested in restoration than retribution. On the
other hand, he or she will not shower others with shallow
praise simply because it is the acceptable thing to do. A
compliment from such a person has substance and significance.

Finally, those who are satisfied with the Lord never
have to lie—even when the reputation of God is at stake.
They will not claim to have all the answers. They will be
better listeners than talkers. Best of all, they won't tell
all they know!

One of the greatest descriptions of our Lord came from
John, who never got over the fact that he was someone
whom Jesus loved. The apostle said that Jesus was "full
of grace and truth" (John 1:14). In today's terms, that
would translate into graciousness and honesty. Grace
without honesty is a travesty; truth without a gracious
spirit can kill. But when both are combined, people will
call us "Christlike"—that is, Christians.

Now, let's don't get discouraged! Remember, we are
still *under construction,* a term popularly used in
cyberspace. It means that there is more to come. As we
commit our speech to the Lord, we will overflow with
wonderful themes. Our tongues will become skillful and
excellent pens, declaring the lovingkindness at dawn and
the faithfulness of God at dusk. Above all, we will find
satisfaction.

Study Questions
Chapter 14 · The Fruit of Our Lips

1. Review the teachings of Jesus about speech and its relationship to our attitudes (hearts).

2. What are the illustrations that the apostle James uses in his letter to describe the tongue? Why did he choose these particular word pictures?

3. Are Christians basically honest? Is honesty automatic, or do we have to work at it? Explain.

4. What does the Bible say about gossip?

5. How can believers be encouraging in their compliments without becoming manipulative, shallow, and flattering?

The Gift of Generosity

Blessed is the man who fears the Lord, who delights greatly in His commandments. His descendants will be mighty on earth; the generation of the upright will be blessed. Wealth and riches will be in his house, and his righteousness endures forever.... He is gracious, and full of compassion, and righteous. A good man deals graciously and lends; he will guide his affairs with discretion. Surely he will never be shaken (Psalm 112:1-6).

Psalm 111 and Psalm 112 date back to some of the earliest times of hymnody. These short poems were written by the same pen. In each the Hebrew phrases are arranged alphabetically. Later, each psalm was divided into the same number of verses. However, there is a thematic difference: Psalm

111 celebrates the character and works of God; Psalm 112 describes the character and generosity of the godly person who has been blessed by the Lord. In *The Treasury of David,* Charles H. Spurgeon suggests the following:

> While the first declares the glory of God, the second speaks of the reflection of the divine brightness in men born from above. God is here praised for the manifestation of his glory which is seen in his people, just as in the preceding Psalm he was magnified for his own personal acts. The hundred and eleventh speaks of the great Father, and this describes his children renewed after his image (Vol. 3, p. 15).

A comparison of Psalms 111 and 112 is given in the following chart:

Psalm 111		Psalm 112
The Glory of God		God's Reflection in a Christian
(The Great Father)		*(Those in His Image)*
"The Lord is gracious and full of compassion."	(v. 4)	God's servant is "gracious, and full of compassion."
"God gives of His abundance to those who fear Him."	(v. 5)	A good man lends to those in need.
God gives His people the nations.	(v. 6)	"The righteous will be in everlasting remembrance."
The precepts of the Lord are sure.	(v. 7)	The heart of the righteous is steadfast.
The Lord "has sent redemption to His people."	(v. 9)	His people give to the poor.

Because the Lord sent redemption to His people, they will give to the poor. As a result, the praise of the Lord endures forever, and the horn (name) of the righteous will be given honor (grateful respect). The point is well made: He who has received God's gracious generosity will find satisfaction in being generous to others. Not only will the believers have chosen a good name, but the name of the Lord will be praised!

Giving to Others

Generosity is giving to others. One of the most generous persons recorded in the Bible was Dorcas. In Acts 9, immediately following the conversion of Saul, the churches experienced peace throughout Galilee, Judea, and Samaria (v. 31). The church was strengthened, and many congregations were planted throughout the area. Peter, the apostle, evangelized the entire region and finally came to Lydda.

While he was there, two men from the church in Joppa asked Peter to come because a woman named Tabitha (*Dorcas* in Greek) had become sick and died. After Peter arrived in Joppa (adjacent to the modern city of Tel Aviv), he immediately went to the upper room where this beloved lady lay. Asking the mourners to leave, he knelt and said, "Tabitha, arise" (v. 40). Dorcas opened her eyes and sat up. Peter took her by the hand, lifted her to her feet, and escorted her to meet her brothers and sisters in the Lord.

Seeing this miracle, many believed. Interestingly, this miracle preceded an even greater event—the pouring out of the Holy Spirit upon the Gentiles.

Note the description the historian Luke gives of Dorcas. She was a Christian woman who was "full of good works and charitable deeds" (Acts 9:36). When Peter arrived, those Dorcas had helped greeted the apostle by showing him the robes and garments she had made for them. Her unselfishness had won their love. She pointed the lost to God by investing in their lives, even when they were unable to repay her.

Dorcas' unselfish benevolence brought great joy to the people. Think of the effort it must have been for the men to travel to Lydda to ask Peter to come to their city. Later, the news of Dorcas' resurrection spread quickly. She was deeply loved and respected by many who without her would not have been reached with the message of the good news. While someone might disagree with your doctrine, he or she cannot ignore your deeds as a loving, caring Christian.

Filled With the Spirit

Generosity accompanies the infilling of the Holy Spirit. In the sixth chapter of Galatians, Paul said it this way:

> And let us not grow weary while doing good, for in due season we shall reap if we do not lose heart. Therefore, as we have opportunity, let us do good to all, especially to those who are of the household of faith (vv. 9, 10).

The apostle had just completed his discussion of the harvest (fruit) of the Spirit (5:22-24), warning those who consider themselves superspiritual to beware of the tendencies to become proud, to compete with each other, and to compare spirituality (5:25, 26).

Paul then lists three characteristics of one who is truly Spirit filled.

- A Spirit-filled believer will be gentle, restoring the fallen in a spirit of kindness (6:1-4).

- A Spirit-filled believer will be generous, sharing not only the Word, but also doing good to others (6:5-10).

- A Spirit-filled believer will glory in the cross of Christ, not in the cost of his or her own sacrifice.

When you meet Christians with these attributes, you identify them as being Christlike . . . and satisfied!

The Ministry of Refreshment

Generosity gives affirmation and encouragement. The ministry of giving and the ministry of encouragement are closely related. Mentioned in the Book of Acts, Barnabas is one of the most unsung heroes in the New Testament. Without him, there probably would not have been a New Testament. It was Barnabas who, following the conversion of Saul (Paul), had the courage to introduce him to the rest of the church (9:27). He even accompanied the apostle on missionary assignments.

This wealthy Cyprian landowner's name meant, "son of encouragement." He was a generous man controlled by the Holy Spirit who was faithful and kind. He was an example of what I like to call "the ministry of refreshment."

Barnabas showed his faith by performance, not pretense, much like Dorcas. He sold his land to assist in meeting fellow believers' needs. In contrast to the offering of Ananias and Sapphira, his gift was honest and sacrificial. It was given in love and set an example for the rest of the early church. Is it any wonder that when God chose Paul, the teacher, to begin the first missionary journey, He also included Barnabas, the giver, as a model. No wonder the first congregations formed were able to become indigenous in such a short period of time. The new believers had not only heard, but they had also seen a pattern to follow.

Barnabas saw what others could do with the gifts God had given them. He believed that Paul's conversion had been genuine, and so was willing to risk his own reputation to sponsor him. He also championed the causes of others like John Mark, defending him before the apostle Paul and insisting on giving the young lad a chance. Time proved Barnabas was right.

Both Barnabas and Dorcas had their focus on people, not on projects or positions. The reason both of these persons are overlooked is that they never sought recognition for themselves. Barnabas was willing for his name to be second to Paul's. He was willing to see others get the credit. The result was that the believers were strengthened and the unsaved were touched. Someone has expressed this truth: "People are attracted more often than they are persuaded."

A Fountain of Blessing

Generosity is a fountain of blessing. An ancient story is told of a man named Abba Agathon who went to town one day to sell some of his wares. On the way he met a crippled man lying on the side of the road. The crippled man asked Abba where he was going. "To town, to sell some things," replied Abba.

"Will you do me a favor and carry me there?" the crippled man requested. So Abba carried him to the town. "Put me down where you sell your wares," said the man. When Abba sold an article, the crippled man asked, "How much did you sell it for?" Abba then told him the price. "Buy me a cake," continued the man, and Abba bought him a cake.

When Abba Agathon had sold all his wares and was ready to leave, the disabled man asked, "Are you going back?"

"Yes," replied Abba. "Then do me the favor of carrying me back to the place where you found me." Once more picking up the crippled man, Abba carried him back to that place.

Then the man said, "Abba Agathon, you are filled with divine blessings in heaven and on earth." Raising his eyes, Agathon saw no man. An angel of the Lord had come to try him.

The writer of Hebrews encourages believers to express brotherly love in tangible ways. He writes . . .

> Be sure to welcome strangers [practice hospitality] into your home. By doing this, some people have welcomed angels as guests, without even knowing it (Hebrews 13:2, *CEV*).

I am not suggesting that we open our doors to everyone who knocks. To do so would be foolish and dangerous. However, God does ask us to consider doing acts of kindness and hospitality that are a sacrifice to us and a blessing to others. If we want the blessing of God, then we must do for others without any expectation of return.

McDonald Madness

Several months ago our youngest son, Derek, and his wife, Sonia, were in the checkout line at a local market. In front of them was a couple who appeared to have been married only a few days. The newlyweds were buying mops, brooms, and other household items that turn the honeymoon into the "money-moon." While the cashier was adding up their bill, the husband turned to his bride and asked, "Do we have enough money to buy supper on the way home?"

"No, Dear," the wife responded. "After this, we are broke."

Derek and Sonia are two of the most gracious and giving people I have ever known. Several evenings a week they serve their families, friends, and others. Their generosity is expressed not only through material gifts, but also through the menial tasks of housework they do. God has given them a special softness. Being softened by the Lord is different from being a "soft touch."

Overhearing the couple's conversation, Derek and Sonia looked at each other, nodded, slipped a $20 bill into the newlyweds' hands, and said, "Here, have a McDonald's madness!" They expected nothing in return except a quiet nod of thanks from the young couple. Suddenly the newlyweds spun around and yelled, "You can't do this! Do you always go around giving money away?"

Everyone in the grocery store turned their attention to

the couple, thinking someone was being robbed or mugged. When the other shoppers heard what happened, they stared in unbelief. Embarrassed at the publicity, Derek and Sonia said, "Take it, and have fun." Amazed, the young couple smiled and went on their way, probably to have a "Big Mac attack."

The story doesn't end there. Following this encounter, Derek and Sonia came to our house. They didn't plan to say anything about the incident, but the glow on their faces and a lightness about their talk caused us to ask what the big announcement was. (No, Sonia was not pregnant.) As they reluctantly shared the events of moments before, it was obvious that they had a sense of blessing and satisfaction the world could not understand.

Kindness Rewarded

Generosity is an act that will be rewarded. In 2 Samuel 9:7, we read of David's kindness to Mephibosheth. (With a name like that, Mephibosheth probably needed all the kindness he could get).

Years before when King Saul had tried to take David's life, the king's son, Jonathan, determined to remain close friends with David. Jonathan recognized that God had chosen the shepherd as king and accepted it as God's will. Later, after Jonathan was killed in battle and David came to power, he wanted to find a way to show generosity to Jonathan's offspring.

David found Mephibosheth, Jonathan's son who was physically disabled and desperately needed help. David welcomed the opportunity to restore all of Saul's land to the young man. He then invited the youth to eat at his table every day. Ordinarily, the heirs of a deposed king were either killed or banished! Having Mephibosheth at his table was David's way of expressing his gratitude for Jonathan's kindness.

Showing kindness, rather than revenge or envy, benefits everyone. The kind acts of Jonathan toward David brought safety to his own descendants long after he was gone. Kindness always leaves its beneficial influence long after the helpful act has been completed. How would David have felt had he shown vengeance on Saul's family instead of kindness? There might have been momentary satisfaction, but it would have eventually resulted in guilt and bitterness. Kind people don't harbor past wrongs, nor do they remain bitter. Instead, they seek to do good even to those who wrong them. When we sow seeds of kindness, we will be repaid in kind . . . sometimes unexpectedly. That is the promise given in Ephesians 6:7, 8:

> With goodwill doing service, as to the Lord, and not to men, knowing that whatever good anyone does, he will receive the same from the Lord, whether he is a slave or free.

The Lollipop

Recently Dr. Vincent R. Bird, a close friend, went to be with the Lord at the age of 83. For nearly 59 years, Vince and his wife, Connie, served as Foursquare ministers—spending nearly two decades of this time as the international director of youth and Christian education of that denomination. Their lives were filled with dedication, humor, and a giving spirit.

One day while they were pastoring in Kansas, their

youngest daughter, Connie Lou, came home with five lollipops. As the young child approached the family table, her father suggested, "Why don't you share one with your mom?" Connie Lou smiled and with extended hand gave a lollipop to her mother.

"How about Dad?" was the next suggestion. The smile remained and the gift made.

"And your oldest brother, Robert?" The smile diminished somewhat, but she continued sharing her bounty with others.

"And your sister, Pat?" Connie Lou began counting the lollipops, but obeyed. There was only one left for her to enjoy.

Then came the ultimate test. "And your brother, Dan?" If she agreed, there would be none left for her. After a time of consideration, the young girl slowly reached out and placed her final lollipop into Dan's hand. At that moment, she had given sacrificially.

As soon as she gave up her final lollipop, everyone in the family extended their hands, giving all the lollipops back to Connie Lou with praise and commendation. Not only had Connie Lou been taught the lesson of sowing and reaping, but she also had the satisfaction of enjoying all the lollipops.

I first heard Dr. Bird tell this story when I was 11 years old. On numerous occasions when I was making major decisions in my ministry, I recalled my friend's conclusion: "You never need to worry about giving all you have to God and to others, because God will reward you with more than you can ever give away." Having been in the ministry for more than 30 years, I understand that the return might not be in material possessions, but in the satisfaction that comes from a generous heart.

When we experience that kind of satisfaction, we will know true satisfaction with God, our highest delight!

Study Questions
Chapter 15 ▪ The Gift of Generosity

1. Why should generosity be natural for a believer in Jesus Christ?

2. What should be the motive for a believer's generosity?

3. Is there a "Dorcas" in your life or church? What distinguishes these types of people?

4. What role did Barnabas play in the early Church? List at least five lessons you could learn from his example.

5. Explain the relationship between being generous and being gentle.

A
Proper View
of
Achievement

He shall be like a tree planted by the rivers of water, that brings forth its fruit in its season, whose leaf also shall not wither; and whatsoever he does shall prosper (Psalm 1:3, see also vv. 1, 2).

This psalm begins with the word, "blessed." In the original text this word had several meanings, implying that the one who delights in the way and the will of the Lord shall be showered with satisfaction. The man who does not walk in the counsel of the ungodly will discover his journey leads through the multitude of blessings which His Lord has planted along the path.

The man who chooses not to stand in the way of sinners will find his identity and security confirmed by achievements which His Lord grants. The man who does not sit in the seat of the scornful will enjoy the fulfillment the Lord delights to make his destiny. Because his delight is in the law of the Lord—not in ungodly counsel—the righteous man not only enjoys God's wisdom, but also His covenant and His fellowship. He is "blessed," as a tree planted by a life-giving stream. This tree, planted so strategically that there is a continual supply of life-giving water, is a tree pruned so that its fullest potential for fruitfulness will be realized, groomed so that its beauty will take on eternal value, and preserved so that it will bring health and happiness to all around it. Who could want anything more?

Looking Back

The year 1990 was difficult for me. I turned 50, the age when you have more chins than sins; when the term "floppy disc" refers more to your physical shape than to your computer; when bedtime reaches single digits; when you engage in great conversation, but then realize there's no one else in the room. It is also at the age of 50 that, if you have not dared before, you look back over your life to review your accomplishments or failures and to anticipate your future. You really desire that the remaining years of your life be meaningful.

This was the year I took a class on leadership emergence at Fuller Theological Seminary, taught by Dr. Robert Clinton. Looking about me at the other students, I realized they could be my children. At the end of the term, "Bobby" Clinton always had the oldest student in the room pray a benediction over the rest of the class. I was so much older than the rest that he allowed me to pray twice!

In the beginning of that same year, God promised me He was going to do something special in my ministry. One evening Bobby talked about a gentleman named Gene Solberg who had been a mentor to him, helping him grow deeper with Christ and giving him direction into the ministry. Almost falling out of my chair, I thought to myself, *I know Gene Solberg!* After class we confirmed the fact that his "Solberg" and mine were indeed the same person. That conversation reminded us of several other believers I had known in the U.S. Air Force while stationed in Japan from 1959 to 1961. What made the moment more significant was the fact that I had not been in touch with any of my former colleagues for 29 years. Later, I had the joy of contacting some of those friends once again. Imagine our delight as we reminisced about the past three decades, recalling God's blessings.

Not surprising after that was the 128-page leadership development study I wrote for that class, recounting the half century of my life. I began that paper with three important desires:

1. To write about the unique graces God had given me—lessons, both positive and negative, that were clearly defined in my own mind and served as a solid foundation for future decision making.

2. To apply those principles in my life so that others would be spared the agonies of defeat and find guideposts to the joys of success in doing God's will.

3. To discover what makes me "tick," by overcoming my insecurities through more than 200 hours of analysis and personal evaluation.

One of the major lessons from that study was a sense

of divine destiny promised to me before I was born. God led my parents and me to California, to the church I presently serve, and gifted me with the skills that are converging into fruitfulness in my family and ministry. Truly, "A man's heart plans his way, but the Lord directs his steps" (Proverbs 16:9).

A proper view of *achievement* will encompass two elements: Divine blessing and divine destiny. These make the difference between achievers and those who truly achieve. Achievers forget where they have come from; those who achieve discover that their present is a compilation of the past. Achievers forget those persons who helped them get where they are today; those who really achieve remember that all promotion comes from the Lord as a result of His faithfulness, as well as of the faithfulness of others who have invested in their lives.

Achievers draw attention to their "doing," while those who truly achieve recognize that their influence emanates out of "being." Achievers take great strides to list their accomplishments, while those who achieve possess a sense of personal unworthiness. Achievers find their satisfaction in seeing the task completed, while those who really achieve discover their greatest fulfillment in people and how they were involved in the process.

Self-gratification may be demanded by the achiever, but those who truly achieve understand that the more the leader's authority and sphere of influence increase, the more he or she is required to become a servant. Jesus said it this way:

> You know that the rulers of the Gentiles lord it over them, and those who are great exercise authority over them. Yet it shall not be so among you; but whoever desires to become great among

you, let him be your servant. And whoever
desires to be first among you, let him be your
slave—just as the Son of Man did not come to
be served, but to serve, and to give His life a
ransom for many (Matthew 20:25-28).

Serving Others

I have mentioned many friends I served with in Northern Japan. A family I have not seen since 1963 is Clyde
and LaRue Wilton. At that time, Clyde was an Air Force
chaplain serving under the endorsement of the Southern
Baptist Convention.

I first met the Wilton family during a Friday night service on Misawa Air Base attended by men and their families from all Evangelical denominations. There was a
special emphasis on music, so Clyde asked me to assume
the responsibility of that ministry. My duties permitted
me enough free time to accept. I also assisted him in
beginning a Bible class in English at a local Baptist church
in the city. As we worked together, I became part of the
Wilton family.

Clyde had studied Greek, and he had recently finished
a translation of the Book of John for the American Bible
Society. He also discovered a common pattern in letter-
writing throughout the Pauline Epistles that I have since
used as a model. He developed the habit of writing one
personal letter each day.

In 1963, however, because of a doctrinal conflict with
the senior chaplain on base, Clyde was passed over a second time for promotion. This event necessitated his retirement
from the Air Force. He returned to Texas where today he

serves as senior pastor of a Baptist congregation in Bryan. Over the years we have corresponded somewhat regularly.

From the natural way of looking at achievement, some might think Clyde had failed. But Clyde's greatest gift was serving as a godly mentor. During the years I was in Japan, I observed that Clyde regularly chose 15 young men and invested himself in their lives during their terms of service. They were from various denominations and had many different callings. To Clyde, this didn't matter. He saw them as people with God's blessings and destiny.

Thirty years later, I contacted many of these men, and found them involved in Christian service—as ministers, missionaries, college professors, denominational and interdenominational representatives, and active lay members in local churches. These disciples are involved in the wide spectrum of the body of Christ, in Evangelical churches, in traditional denominations, and in Pentecostal or Charismatic congregations. Not one has ceased his commitment to the Lord or his dedication to serving others.

The achievements of Clyde and LaRue Wilton have caused magnified ripples of the grace of God to flow around the world. Their lives have been multiplied thousands of times over, simply because they followed the model of Jesus. They learned that serving others was the way of receiving fulfillment.

A Great Achiever

The Reverend Bernie Quimby served as a Pentecostal preacher for many years. Because God led him to shepherd smaller congregations, Bernie had to be a tentmaker—a minister who also practiced another trade. No matter what needed fixing in a home or a large office building, he knew how to do it. For many years following his retirement from the pastorate, he served as head of maintenance at the facilities of our denominational headquarters. His responsibilities included the care and upkeep of 70 other properties as well. Until his death from cancer in February 1991, Bernie was the one to call if you were ever in need, spiritually or materially. To those who did not have the privilege of getting to know him intimately, Bernie would seem to be just a nice fellow who had served Jesus the best he could.

But Bernie achieved! Whether in the hearts of the hundreds he won to the Lord in his five decades of ministry, or in the heart of my teenage son whom he took under his wings to teach the "art of maintenance," Bernie understood true achievement. It was my privilege at his memorial service on February 21, 1991, to share the following poem:

> *What is it in the heart of a man that makes*
> *him stand above the rest?*
> *Is it courage or wisdom, or even stature*
> *that helps him meet the test?*
> *Is it found in seats of honor,*
> *or in pursuit of might?*
> *Oh, rare are those who find it,*
> *who on its wings alight.*
> *For greatness is not found in*
> *valiant acts or deeds,*
> *But in the tenderness of hearts*
> *that see the other's needs.*
>
> *It reaches out in calloused hands,*
> *worn by a full day's toil,*
> *To touch the wounded souls of men,*

with the health of heaven's oil;
It weeps with those who dare to weep,
and smiles with those who smile;
It takes the time to lend an ear, to walk the second mile.
No, grand acts are not done with fanfare from above,
But with the touch of caring hands,
outstretched in quiet love.

Humble men with faithful hands,
changed by the grace of God,
Will always rise above the rest to
walk where few have trod.
But as they climb the peaks of faith,
they do not walk alone,
For they bring so many with them,
those that they have known.
No, glory is not measured in
gold or goods of men,
But in the treasure of grateful
hearts to whom they've been a friend.

By Ron Williams
In Memory of the Reverend Bernard Quimby
February 21, 1991

A True Elder

Some years ago, I was asked to speak in Calgary, Alberta, Canada, at the Canadian National Foursquare Convention. Many of these Foursquare pastors had been our mentors when Carole and I first entered the ministry. Now, I was returning as a representative of our denomination's U.S. Board of Directors.

The task ahead was great. As I viewed the magnificence of the Canadian Rockies, I broke out in a cold sweat and asked the Lord, "How can I perform my eldership responsibilities to those who were my teachers? I don't know how to act as an elder!"

Inside I heard a whisper, "Ron, you don't have to do anything! You *are* an elder, an older brother." Then I understood that achievement is not in positional authority, but in personal relationships. Eldership was not what I had *achieved*; an elder was someone I had *become*.

When we understand God's perspective on achievement—our becoming all that God has designed and destined us to be—we take giant steps toward becoming satisfied. True achievement happens within. Psalm 1 declares that when the law of God becomes the inner vitality of life's tree, then our fruitfulness will be seasonable, bringing life to others. Our leaf—the beauty of God's character in us and the credibility of our lifestyle—will be maintained by God!

What has God designed you to be? Remember the first session in Bobby Clinton's class? Take out a piece of paper and draw a tombstone. Now, from your heart, write your epitaph. How would you want others to describe you? Would you have them talk about your mighty deeds? Would you have them list the positions you have held? Or would you hope they would describe *you*, not your deeds?

Each day you are adding another letter to your epitaph. Each step can be bring you closer to that desired description becoming a reality in your life. God grant that your greatest "achievement" will be that you were satisfied with Him, Your highest delight!

Study Questions
Chapter 16 · A Proper View of Achievement

1. In your own words, contrast the "achiever" and one who truly contributes to the lives of others.

2. Discuss the various Biblical passages regarding servanthood.

3. What do we mean when we say, "Ministry emanates out of being"? What is the relationship of character to giftedness?

4. Make a list of the "Clyde Wiltons" and "Bernie Quimbys" you know. Take the opportunity to express your appreciation to them.

5. From this chapter, state three important truths the Lord is presently speaking to you.

Chapter 17

Looking
to the
Hills

I will lift up my eyes to the hills—from whence comes my help? My help comes from the Lord, who made heaven and earth. . . . He who keeps you will not slumber. . . . The Lord is your keeper; the Lord is your shade. . . . The Lord shall preserve you . . . your soul . . . your going out and your coming in . . . forevermore (Psalm 121:1-8).

Possibly no other psalm written brings such comfort and hope as this "Song of Ascents." As one reads, he gets the feeling of pilgrimage, of travel. Psalm 121 is the song of a traveler making his climb out of a valley toward the summit where rest awaits. The journey is not easy. The heat of the day and the perils of sleeping in the tented fields at night take their toll.

Those who are weak lift up their eyes, wishing that this part of the journey were already ended. Those who have fallen prey to marauders lift up their eyes, knowing that safety is to be found at their destination. In either case, there is no option but to continue the trek upward, one step at a time.

Sojourners and Pilgrims

Some expositors feel that this song describes the ascent that pilgrims made toward the city of Jerusalem to celebrate the feasts or to worship at the Temple. On the last evening of their journey, in view of the mountains of Jerusalem and with the journey's end in sight, they rejoiced in their preservation by the One who neither slumbers (becomes too exhausted) nor sleeps (is unavailable to help us).

I recently stood on the summit overlooking the ancient road that leads "up" from Jericho to Jerusalem. Within the course of 25 miles, the Jericho Road climbs from 1,300 feet below sea level to the Holy City which rests on the summit, 2,500 feet above sea level. Also known as the "Valley of the Shadow," the road winds between cliff-like walls of rock and sand, with few trees for shade or protection from the elements or from enemies. Depending on the speed of travel, as well as the load their animals were carrying, the caravan would make this climb over a period lasting up to several days. And I'm sure there were times when they wondered if they would ever make it. Above all, they would never want to make that trip alone. Remember the story of the Good Samaritan?

While standing above that barren ascent, I looked

southwest and noticed that in the distance one could see the hilltop of Bethany, across the Kidron Valley from Jerusalem. What a refreshing sight that must have been to those who had journeyed from afar. There truly was an end to their arduous journey. Once they could see their destination, they no longer counted the steps it would take to arrive.

A thousand years later, the apostle Peter was writing to a group of sojourners and pilgrims. And the spiritual steps they were taking were just as perilous and demanding. Their adversaries were not the elements of nature or the thieves who waited in ambush to steal their earthly goods. Their suffering was from the Enemy of their souls and from those who through extreme persecution sought to steal life and faith from them. Rather than directing their attention to a city, the patriarch of the church pointed the pilgrims to the Creator-Savior: "Therefore let those who suffer according to the will of God commit their souls to Him in doing good, as to a faithful Creator" (1 Peter 4:19). From where would their help come? From the very crest of Mt. Calvary.

The People of God

The word *therefore* implies that much had already been said to bring the readers to such a conclusion. Actually, Peter began this part of the discussion in Chapter 3 when he wrote . . .

> And who is he who will harm you if you become followers of what is good? But even if you should suffer for righteousness' sake, you are blessed. "And do not be afraid of their threats, nor be troubled" (vv. 13, 14).

193

Pressure or suffering will reveal the people of God. Their reaction to distress and difficult times will be seen in stark contrast to that of the unsaved. The believer will see suffering as a privilege: "You are blessed." They will not panic in terror, as an animal that is caged during a time of fire or calamity. On the contrary, those who look to the preeminence of God will be full of hope, and in meekness and humility will be able to adequately explain their peace (v. 15). Their composure will make the world envious and curious, startling it by the quality of their behavior (v.16).

Ouch! This is where I am the most vulnerable. When problems arise, the first thing to go is my positive outlook. Entering as it leaves are depression, complaining, and all kinds of erratic actions. The result is that I do not act any differently than nonbelievers, who having seen my chaos, respond, "I don't need to accept Christ; I've got enough problems already!" Yes, the world and God are watching. How impressed are they?

Peter also cautions that we be sure that the suffering we experience comes because of our well-doing, not because of our worldly sinfulness or lack of due diligence.

The Purpose of God

Pressure or suffering reveals the purpose of God (1 Peter 3:18–4:1). Throughout his letter, there is one thing that never ceases to amaze the apostle: the extent of Christ's tremendous willingness to suffer and die for him. Never losing a sense of awesomeness of this, Peter gives us five purposes for our Lord's suffering.

1. *Christ died to bring us to God (v. 18).* His purpose

in dying was that unjust men and women would once again turn their faces toward God and be reconciled to Him. In the same way, it is amazing how quickly suffering or crises turns our eyes once again toward the hills . . . and to God.

2. *Christ died to experience fuller life (v. 18).* Though He was slain by sinful men, His body did not rest in the grave as those of others. He was quickened by the Holy Spirit into a new dynamic dimension of resurrected life. Wow, what we become, simply because we have grown through the difficult times! Could it be that one of the purposes of God's allowing us to go through the "valley of the shadow" was to bring us into a fuller dimension of life with Him?

3. *Christ died to pronounce victory over Satan (vv. 19, 20).* This portion of scripture is difficult to understand until one sees that the word *preached* was not related to evangelism but to sentencing. It carries the idea of a courtroom where the verdict is read. In Romans 16, the apostle Paul assures the church in Rome that they would "crush Satan" under their feet (v. 20). How was this to come about? I have an idea that it came mainly through perseverance in suffering.

4. *Christ died to make possible the resurrection (vv. 20, 21).* In the same way that the ark built by Noah rode through the storm successfully, Christ was declared to be the Son of God through the resurrection and His glorification. So is our hope and confidence stabilized by the pressures that come our way. Suffering prepares us to leave this world.

5. *Christ died to intercede on behalf of men (v. 22).* Because Christ died, rose, and lives at the right hand of

God with all authority, He constantly ministers and intercedes on our behalf. In like manner, the challenges which we have been forced to face prepare us to minister to others.

Turning us back to God, bringing us to a new dimension of spiritual life, making us victorious over Satan, preparing us for the world that is to come, and providing us with the experience and wisdom needed to minister to others—if these are what suffering produces, then we can find satisfaction, even amid the most extreme difficulties.

Suffering reveals the power of God. Suffering is valuable only when it results in growth within the believer. The believer should use such occasions to reckon himself dead to sin (4:1, 2). When pressure or suffering hits, we will be confronted with two choices: to look upon it as a chance to follow God's pattern, or to react just like everyone else. Peter advised not to even think about the latter, for it has no power over us unless we allow it. Rather, consider ourselves alive to God so that His strength may be revealed in our weaknesses.

When confronted with a difficult situation the believer should not allow himself to slip back into the old way of coping (4:3-5). When he acts according to God's pattern, he might be considered foolish. But remember that God will bring those who accuse into judgment. The believer should also control his emotions (vv. 6, 7), looking to the nearness of Christ's return.

Intemperance or conceit should never be allowed to overwhelm his objectivity. He must be ruled by God's feelings, not his own.

The Power of God

Finally, the believer should be strengthened through watchfulness in prayer (4:6, 7). As he penned this, Peter probably had in mind the night he failed to pray with Christ and was thus unable to withstand temptation. Actually in all of the areas above, he had failed miserably. But what had changed his way of responding? The patient lessons of experience and the power of God.

May Hung served as my personal secretary in Hong Kong for 15 years. Her mother had died when May and her sister, Susannah, were quite young. Her father, a Buddhist, was a loving but very strict man who blamed the "council of the ancestors" for robbing him of the love of his life. When May accepted Jesus into her life in 1970, not only did he consider her decision a betrayal of his faith but also a refusal to worship or honor her mother.

Despite all her efforts to convince him of her love and respect, for the next nine years this young lady experienced tremendous rejection, as well as emotional and physical abuse. When her sister, Susanna, found Jesus, matters became worse. His anger was poured out even more adamantly.

No matter what her father did, May's response was that she loved Jesus, she loved her family, and above all, she was willing to receive whatever he wanted to do to her. At times, the cost of such a commitment was great. She was often criticized by other believers and told she shouldn't take such a submitted posture toward him. She "ought to obey God rather than men," was the scripture most often quoted . . . and most often misused.

As a result of her Christlike response, however, a decade later her father came to know Jesus just weeks before he passed away from cancer. What convinced "Papa" Hung that Jesus was the answer to his eternity was his daughter's adherence to Peter's principles.

The Protection of God

Suffering reveals the protection of God. As we see others experiencing the processing of God through crises times, it impacts both our relationships (vv. 8, 9) and our stewardship (vv. 10, 11). Regarding our relationships, we must maintain loving forgiveness and show hospitality without complaining. When pressure hits, people fail, and our natural tendency is to condemn and criticize. But when a person is down, he doesn't need to be hit again. He needs loving understanding.

We also need to remain alert to the needs of others. Those who suffer or who are going through hard times need Christian friends with whom they can fellowship and be able to express themselves without fear of judgment. Suffering may cause great inconvenience, but we must be careful not to complain.

It is vital that our spiritual gifts be combined with other believers' so that we might give full support to one another. Peter says that whether it be those who speak or those who serve, God must be the one glorified and honored.

The Processing of God

Suffering reveals the processing of God. In bringing

the matter to a practical conclusion, some misconceptions must be confronted. Suffering in the believer's life is natural (v. 12). It should never be seen as strange or unusual. Above all, when one goes through such times, he should never look at the experience as if God were testing him with an eye to judgment. But just as in school, his exams provide the opportunity to pass the test and graduate to a higher level. When discussing testing I usually tell people I have good news and I have bad news. The good news is that God will bring us through our trials with flying colors. The bad news is that He is simply qualifying us to undergo pressure at an even higher level.

Suffering in the believer's life brings forth fruit (v. 13). It produces in us a joy which was Christ's. It works a much greater purpose than you or I can ever imagine. Have you ever gone through a hard time when you really wondered if there was enough strength to manage? You may even have questioned the Lord regarding His love, His reason, and His wisdom. Then, years later, as you looked back, you smiled, seeing the total picture much more clearly. You are literally amazed at how wise the Lord was all along.

Contrary to the belief of many, suffering in the believer's life is spiritual (vv. 14-16). The apostle confidently stated that "the Spirit of glory and of God rests upon you." You never need to be ashamed as long as you are not suffering because you are a murderer, a thief, an evil doer, or—I wish I didn't have to include this—a busybody.

Christ's Pruning

Suffering in the believer's life is necessary (vv. 17-19).

Christ's pruning will begin in us. The difficult times make us fit for His presence. They place our focus fully on His faithfulness, not on our frailty. Unfortunately, while rejoicing in His faithfulness as our Savior, we fail to rejoice in His faithfulness as our Creator. Too few of us recognize that He who creates is also under obligation to sustain and bring that which He has created to its completion and fulfillment.

It was Marcel Proust who said, "We are healed of suffering only by experiencing it in full." John Powell put it this way: "By afflictions God is spoiling us of what otherwise might have spoiled us. When he makes the world too hot for us to hold, we let it go." The Chinese say, "The gem cannot be polished without friction, nor man perfected without trials."

"You ought to do something about these pews, Pastor" startled me from my Saturday evening prayer time in the church sanctuary. More than that, my recognition of the voice even more surprised me. For months I had been trying to reach Gerhard Schultz, who desperately needed the Lord. Our ministry had touched his wife and five children, but he was a tough nut to crack.

"Well, why don't you do it for me?" I replied. In addition to his normal vocation, this 35-year-old German was an excellent carpenter. As he continued talking, however, I quickly realized that though he would have given everything to do so, he would be in no shape to help.

"I thought I'd find you here. I need your help. I've just found out I have cancer and have nowhere to turn. Please help!" His bulky frame concealed the devastating disease that was already ravaging his body. Over the months that followed as I visited this friend who gave his life to the Lord in the hospital, I watched as his body deteriorated into a mass of skin and skeleton.

As a church and as individuals, we prayed, believed, and asked God for a miracle. Gerhard prayed and grew immensely in his knowledge of God's promises and in faith. It seemed that the more ill he became, the stronger his understanding of the ways of the Lord grew. We claimed the promises of God and held tightly to the conviction that it is God's will to heal. We were believing for a miracle.

Then came the day when Gerhard, knowing that his time on earth was nearing the end, asked me to drive him home from the hospital so he could spend three hours with his wife and children. He was fully aware that this was to be his last opportunity to be with them on earth. I will never forget my feelings, which ranged from anxiety at being an invited observer of the family's last moments together to anger with God for allowing this to take place.

I asked to be excused while Gerhard said his final goodbyes, and fifteen minutes later as we helped him into the car, he simply said, "Take me home!" His eyes were wet with sorrow, yet there was a gleam that assured me that he had a bright future just ahead. A few days later, I conducted the funeral for this man who was now enjoying his faith to the fullest and was totally healed.

During his nine months of suffering, Gerhard and I often talked about the will of the Lord. We dared to open a theological Pandora's box and ask why God would allow someone to suffer. There was a discussion of why God delivered Peter out of prison when He allowed James to be beheaded (Acts 12). Does suffering include sickness, as well as persecution? Needless to say, our limited understanding was exceeded by the eternal purposes of God. We came to the conclusion that God's ways are eternal and much wiser than ours.

But there was one conclusion that we vowed to preserve: "For I have learned in whatever state I am, to be content [satisfied]" (Philippians 4:11). For Paul, "whatever state" included labor, beatings, imprisonments, stonings, shipwrecks, long journeys, danger of every sort, weariness, hunger and thirst, fastings, cold and nakedness, infirmities, reproaches, needs, persecutions and distresses. Oh yes, on top of that was the care of the churches. And then there was possibly a problem with the apostle's eyesight, and so forth. But that which allowed him to "do all things through Christ who strengthens me" (Philippians 4:13) was the fact that the apostle did not major on his need, but centered his attention on learning to be satisfied.

The Foundation of Satisfaction

I flee from the debates which try to lay the blame either on God's will or man's faith, or lack thereof. Nor is there any credence given or help found in our pat answers. The foundation of our satisfaction, even amid suffering is . . .

> All things work together for good to those who *love* God, to those who are the called according to His purpose. . . . Who shall separate us from the *love* of Christ? Shall tribulation, or distress, or persecution, or famine, or nakedness, or peril, or sword? . . . In all these things we are more than conquerors through Him who *loved* us. . . . [Nothing] shall be able to separate us from the

love of God which is in Christ Jesus our Lord (Romans 8:28, 35, 37, 39).

All that truly matters is that God loves us, and we love Him. And it was the brother of James the Beheaded who later wrote, "There is no fear [*phobia*] in love; but perfect [*teleios*—matured and completed] love casts out fear. ... We love Him because He first loved us" (1 John 4:18, 19).

No matter the results, I will still preach the healing power of Christ. For every need, I will pray with conviction and with confidence that God will answer supernaturally. In every situation, I will still believe that "He who is in [me] is greater than he who is in the world" (1 John 4:4). Whatever the balance of my bank account, God still wants me to prosper and be in health, even as my soul prospers (3 John 1:2). I have both been destined and designed to overcome and, most of all, to be satisfied . . .

> For He Himself has said, "I will never leave you nor forsake you." So we may boldly say: "The Lord is my helper; I will not fear. What can man do to me? . . . Jesus Christ is the same yesterday, today, and forever (Hebrews 13:5, 6, 8).

Jesus was David's keeper; He will be mine. Jesus was David's shade; He will be mine. Jesus was David's preserver; He will be mine—for all eternity.

Study Questions
Chapter 17 · Looking to the Hills

1. Do most believers really consider themselves as pilgrims? How has the world's consumerism impacted the Christian's worldview?

2. Consider the value of pressure and tension in the development of Christian character and satisfaction.

3. From 1 Peter 3:18–4:1, write your own "theology of suffering."

4. How does suffering fit together with God's covenant of provision and promises of prosperity?

5. How does suffering produce joy? Is there a difference between believing Romans 8:28 and becoming a fatalist?

A
Heritage
for the
Generations

Blessed is the man who fears the Lord, who delights greatly in His commandments. His descendants will be mighty on earth; the generation of the upright will be blessed (Psalm 112:1, 2).

The father of the righteous will greatly rejoice, and he who begets a wise child will delight in him. Let your father and mother be glad, and let her who bore you rejoice (Proverbs 23:24).

When I was considering writing, I asked a close friend what I should write. His reply was, "Write what you know about." Thus these chapters contain personal illustrations of personal acquaintances, most of them family. In Chapter 11, I discussed the principles of Ephesians 5 and 6 regarding the importance of the family during a time of personal turmoil.

Family Heirlooms

I have three possessions of great value. They are remembrances of my father, whose character and life greatly shaped my theology—my perception of what my heavenly Father must be like. Each of us has some family heirlooms that have been passed down through the generations. A ring, a trumpet, and a Bible are my treasures.

For every major family event, I wear the Williams' family ring. Made of the gold from my parents' wedding rings, the ring is designed with a large "W" surrounded by birthstones of my sisters and me. Unless the Lord comes before I go to be with Him at the end of my life, that ring will be passed on to my oldest grandson. He will carry on our family name. The ring reminds our family of God's destiny for each of us.

My trumpet's valves are all stuck, but from time to time I take it out, dust it off, and remember that my first horn was purchased for me from a small estate left to our family by my maternal grandfather. My mother and dad wanted me to serve the Lord through music, and at age 11, I began to "toot my own horn." Now, two of my sons play trumpets, one plays a guitar, and all three write music. The trumpet is a reminder to our family of God's gifts in our lives. This horn will be passed down to the first child of my third son.

When I was a few days old, I was presented with a small book, an eight-page *Life of Christ*—my first Bible. Each time I pick up this little book, I am reminded of

God's faithfulness. God fulfilled my mother's request, and He fulfilled His covenant with our family. At her dedication, this past summer, I announced that the daughter of my second son would be the recipient of this family heirloom.

Passing on reminders of God's destiny, gifts, and faithfulness to our family is very important. When we reach the end of life's journey, the greatest satisfaction of all will be our families. Do we realize that they are the only possessions we have that we can take to heaven with us?

The Family

Although he never married, the apostle Paul believed in families. He spoke of the church as a family. Most of his letters begin and end with greetings to families and extended households. Even more amazing, these are usually described in terms of relationship rather than position.

In 1 Corinthians 16:15-18, Paul spoke about the household of Stephanas. He made three major observations regarding their family:

1.   They were the "firstfruits of Achaia."

2.   Their home was the center of evangelism.

3.   Stephanas' family was full of purpose.

Paul said they devoted themselves to serving the saints. The term *devoted* literally means "addicted." This family became as committed to serving, as one who comes under the influence of alcohol or drugs. How refreshing to find those who literally crave the opportunity of blessing others!

The family of Stephanas lived interdependently by supplying what was lacking in the lives of other Corinthian believers. The members of the family discovered the value of giving and found freedom in the abandonment of themselves to Christ's people.

Stephanas, Fortunatus, and Achaicus were refreshing. They were valuable to others. Paul writes that they should be acknowledged, because they deserved recognition.

Over the years, I have defined the goal of the pastor or missionary in this way: "To enter into such a sympathetic understanding with the people you shepherd in any culture, so that you might have the opportunity and ability to show them what Christ can mean to them in their circumstances."

Whether in a home with both parents or in a single-parent family, the greatest contribution toward a sense of spiritual satisfaction in our children and our succeeding generations is showing them what Christ has done in our own lives.

A Spiritual Heritage

How can we encourage satisfaction with God in our families, especially when so many other voices clamor for their attention? Succeeding as the head of the family is not providing our children with those things we *didn't* have, but providing them with the spiritual heritage we *do* have.

Our children need a parent—not a professional. Success is usually measured by today's standard in terms of accomplishment. Often from birth, our children are indoctrinated by our examples and expressions with the fallacy that worth comes through position, performance or recognition. What a child needs most is a mother and father who give him a sense of identity so that he will know who he is.

Our children need our presence—not our presents. Because of what we think is economic necessity, we place our children in nursery and preschool. Then when they become school age, the educational authorities become their mentors. Even in the church, children seldom participate with their parents in worship. Then we become concerned and wonder why the values we were taught have not been passed down. The question is not, What is this world coming to? but rather, Where have the parents gone?

Our children need our time—not our treasures. One thing that can never be regained is the time lost in not being with our children while they are still at home. Expensive gifts will never make up for wonderful memory moments shared with your children, and later with their children. Establishing family traditions through the years is one way you will bless future generations.

Our children need our perspective—not perfection. They don't need to make the honor roll at school as much as to be taught how to make honorable decisions. Such lessons are not taught in classrooms, but are caught from a parent who dares to establish a worldview based on God's view and then—in all circumstances—to follow that Biblical worldview. Children also need the freedom to establish their own perspectives, with the guidance of Mom and Dad. Children are blessed when parents don't demand perfection.

Our children need our honesty—not heroism. One of my favorite advertisements on television is about the fellow with a sore muscle who, on the last play of the game, comes off the bench to kick a 14-yard field goal and wins the game in front of a small group of supporters. He tells the story five years later: the kick has become 30 yards, it was raining, and he did it with a pulled ligament in front of 3,000 people. Ten years later: the kick has now become 50 yards, it was in the middle of a blizzard, Dad kicked it with a broken leg while being supported by crutches, and the 80,000 fans carried him off the field. The final scene shows Dad's friends telling the story while the kids are mouthing it in the background. Remember, Dad, if you are too perfect, how can your kids ever end up being as good as you?

Our children need our example—not our expectations. Frankly, I'm glad I grew up when I did. Seeing what my sons had to face when they went through school, I realize that peer pressure has become almost unbearable. Now, a decade later, I cannot fathom what it must be like to go through a metal detector to get to class and then to be surrounded by every type of worldly philosophy and its demand for social acceptability. Add to these influences the violence and eroticism seen on television and in the movies and imagine the dissonance. Our kids are not looking for any more demands; they are looking for an example to follow. Parents, if we don't provide that example, the world will!

Our children need principles—not permission. In a recent survey from the Gallup Poll for Princeton University Research Center, the great majority of youth today cited the lack of parameters for discipline at home as the primary cause of their generation's lack of moral principles. While my sons were growing up, how many times did I hear them say, "Boy, when I have kids, I won't be so strict." What is funny (now, not then) is that they are now talking and acting just like their father, even using the same words! You will never receive the respect of your children if you don't set boundaries for them. Of course, it will be even worse for you and your children if you don't stay within those boundaries yourself.

The Challenge of Parenthood

Raising children is demanding, yet it is worth the effort. Some days can be downright frustrating. One father said, "Our son gets up with the sun. As soon as it shines in his window, he jumps out of bed. Unfortunately, his bedroom window faces west." A mother observed, "I have my doubts about solar energy. My sons stay outside in the sun all day. But when they come in, not one of them has an ounce of energy."

The next time you feel like calling it quits as a parent, just remember that your little girl is innocence playing in the mud; beauty standing on its head; and motherhood dragging a doll by the foot. She is really becoming what you are investing in her.

Some years ago the son of an acquaintance strayed from the ways of the Lord and from the calling God had placed upon him. The despair of the father was immense. Each time the son called home, all Dad wanted to do was preach to him. There was little movement in the son toward repentance until Dad finally listened to Mom, who wisely advised him to, "Just shut up and pray."

Fourteen months later the telephone rang. It was the son calling with the good news that he had renewed his relationship with the Lord and was returning to God's plan for his life. Today, that son is helping other parents and children relate to God and to each other.

Hearing the wonderful news about his son's restoration, the father began to cry with joy, thanking God for being patient and gracious. Then, in that still small voice, God whispered, "Do you remember the day you dedicated your son to me?"

"Yes."

"Were you serious about what you were doing?"

"Yes, Lord, I was." Back came the words, "So was I."

There is nothing as effective in destroying your satisfaction as family difficulty. Remember the vows you made during your wedding? As the two of you partook of communion and asked God to be head of your home, He was more serious even than you were in accepting His part in the responsibility of that covenant. Later, when you dedicated your children and asked Him to cover them with His grace, He really did hear. He will chase them all the days of their lives.

THE LEGACY

The old man looks to the mountain before him—
To climb had been the command;
To conquer, the challenge.
Taking his child by the hand, with the words,
"God will provide,"
He follows the path of obedience
Which leads to the place of sacrifice.
As nightfall comes, father and son halt their steps:

Rest would be needed;
New direction to be heeded;
Also a time to remember the promise,
"A father of many nations,
As the stars in the heavens above,
And the sands of the earth below."

Reaching the summit, the end of their test,
A lamb is provided;
A legacy passed—
Blessing family, tribe, and generations
With the light of faith, the lift of hope
And the lessons of a father's love.

True inheritance is not wrapped
In the foil of possessions
Or in the folly of success;
But is found in daring to dream the impossible,
With faith in God's Son
And fervency in God's service.

A father's portion:
Climbing the mountains of obedience,
Building altars of sacrifice.
A father's example:
Integrity with intensity;
Conviction with tenderness.

Abraham and Isaac; a father and his family;
Patriarch and priest;
Provider yet friend.
And when the mountain has been conquered,
the offering accepted,
His children will still call him "Daddy;"
Their children will call him "blessed."

—Ron Williams
August 4, 1991

Study Questions
Chapter 18 • A Heritage for the Generations

1. What spiritual lessons do your family heirlooms convey?

2. In this computer age, how do you maintain and foster family core values and traditions?

3. Contrast your home with that of Stephanas. Do you have a "family ministry philosophy"?

4. In a world marked by dysfunction, how critical is the need for a Biblical family model? How can you bring order to a dysfunctional home?

5. How should parents respond when their children, at home or away, begin to stray from the paths they have been taught?

Chapter 19

Fully Satisfied

As for me, I will see Your face in righteousness;
I shall be satisfied when I awake in Your likeness
(Psalm 17:15).

An interesting story is told of the famous Sistine Chapel. While Michelangelo artfully painted, the pope occasionally interrupted the work, demanding that the scaffolding be removed so that he could see the glowing colors being laid onto the fresco and its surroundings. The pope was so intrigued by the artistry of this genius that he could not wait until the painting was finished to admire both its brilliance and the matchless skill of Michelangelo.

Imagine the excitement the evening before the masterpiece was completed. There would have been poles, ropes that held them in place, lime and mortar, paint and boards.

Canvas and rubbish littered the floor. There were last minute additions and alterations. Emotions soared as the artist completed his five-year project of love. Yet to those who did not know better, that last day was no different than any other day.

Finally the long-awaited day arrived. Perhaps it went like this: the pope entered the chapel with his beloved Michelangelo and looked to the ceiling. It must have appeared that the roof was missing and he could see the very courts of heaven with the angels singing a triumphant song.

Michelangelo bowed and asked, "Are you satisfied with my work?" With a tear in his eye, a song in his heart, and maybe even his hands upraised, the Pope responded, "I am satisfied. Fully satisfied!"

Psalm 17 portrays a struggle. David pleaded for God's satisfaction. God had tested his heart, placed him before the court of heaven and found nothing evil. David prayed for God's loving-kindness to protect him from his enemies. He declared that he knew the inheritance and treasure of evil men would only be in this life.

As a finale to his life, however, David stated that his inheritance was far beyond the boundaries of this world. When he awoke in the presence of God, not only would God be satisfied, but the king would also!

Our Inheritance

Likewise, whatever fulfillment we have enjoyed while serving the Lord on this earth will never be able to compare with what we will know when God shows us the inheritance He has prepared. When He asks, "Do you like it?" we will only be able to whisper in our new heavenly tongue, "Oh, yes!"

The apostle Paul writes . . .

> For I consider that the sufferings of this present time are not worthy to be compared with the glory which shall be revealed in us (Romans 8:18).

> Therefore we do not lose heart. . . . For our light affliction, which is but for a moment, is working for us a far more exceeding and eternal weight of glory, while we do not look at the things which are seen, but at the things which are not seen. For the things which are seen are temporary, but the things which are not seen are eternal. For we know that if our earthly house, this tent, is destroyed, we have a building from God, a house not made with hands, eternal in the heavens. For in this we groan, earnestly desiring to be clothed with our habitation. . . . Now He who has prepared us for this very thing is God, who also has given us the Spirit as a guarantee [down payment, earnest] (2 Corinthians 4:16-5:2, 5).

Note the contrasts: Sufferings turn into glory; light afflictions turn into immense glory. A moment of pressure becomes an eternity of pleasure; an indestructible tent becomes a heavenly building which will never be destroyed.

We have received only a down payment on what the Holy Spirit wants to give us; in heaven we will receive the entire package! Who wouldn't be satisfied with that! That is why we must not lose heart now.

Mr. Mui's Blessing

"Dad, why does someone have to die on Resurrection [Easter] Sunday?" asked 9-year-old Scott. I was amazed at my son's question.

We had just received word that Mr. Mui, a member of one of our churches in Hong Kong, had died early that Easter morning, 1972. What made it even more shocking was that our entire family had attended a special gathering at the gentleman's home the evening before. The gathering had been a "thanksgiving service" for Mr. Mui's resurrection!

Yes, resurrection. Six weeks earlier, I had received a telephone call from Mr. Mui's daughter, informing me that her 65-year-old father had suffered a severe heart attack and was dying in the hospital. As the Chinese pastor and I prepared to leave for the hospital, a second phone call came. The message was that Mr. Mui had died.

We decided to go on to the hospital anyway to comfort the family. We hailed a taxi (the most convenient form of travel in the colony) and asked the driver to take us to the hospital as quickly as possible.

Suddenly, I received a witness in my heart that Mr. Mui would be sitting upright and eating lunch when we arrived at the hospital. The more I tried to dismiss this illogical thought, the stronger it became. I did not tell the pastor beside me.

We arrived at Queen Elizabeth Hospital, paid the cab, and hastily walked up the stairs to the third room ward. Nearing the room of our brother, I slowed to a snail's pace, wrestling with the thoughts in my mind. I asked the pastor to remain behind while I stuck my head through the door to see the family. Rather than tears of sorrow, I saw tears of joy. Instead of consolation, they needed calming!

My unbelieving eyes (though I had been adequately warned) saw Mr. Mui sitting up in bed, eating a bowl of rice porridge. I asked to see his chart and his doctor. Both confirmed that he had been physically dead for almost 10 minutes. A week later, Mr. Mui was released from the hospital and told to rest.

On the evening of Palm Sunday, Mr. Mui telephoned his pastor and asked that a "thanksgiving service" be held in his home. He was emphatic about the time. It had to be the Saturday night before Easter. We tried to dissuade him about the time, but there was no relenting on his part. Finally, we agreed.

More than twenty people attended the service, including Mr. Mui's grown children. We sang hymns, and our brother shared his testimony. With alarming clarity he warned the members of his family to get right with God. According to him, this message was the reason God had brought him back to life. He then thanked us for coming, prayed for us, and invited us to share tea and rice cakes. Mr. Mui gave our sons special attention, patting their blonde heads and pronouncing a blessing over them.

The telephone call came the next morning, just as we were beginning a sunrise service at the church.

How did I answer Scott's question? Taking his little hands in mine, I answered, "Because the very reason Jesus rose from the dead was so that we would no longer have to worry about dying on Resurrection Sunday. There is no reason to fear because when we believe in Jesus, the *worst* thing that can happen to us is that we go to heaven."

He shook his head in agreement and said, "I see." He then went out to play with his brother.

May we never forget the reason Jesus rose from the dead.

> But now Christ is risen from the dead, and has become the firstfruits of those who have fallen asleep. For since by man came death, by Man also came the resurrection of the dead. For as in Adam all die, even so in Christ all shall be made alive. . . . Behold, I tell you a mystery: We shall not all sleep, but we shall all be changed—in a moment, in the twinkling of an eye, at the last trumpet. For the trumpet will sound, and the dead will be raised incorruptible, and we shall be changed. For this corruptible must put on incorruption, and this mortal must put on immortality. . . . Then shall be brought to pass the saying that is written: "Death is swallowed up in victory." "O Death, where is your sting? O Hades, where is your victory?". . . "Therefore . . . be steadfast, immovable, always abounding in the work of the Lord, knowing that your labor is not in vain (1 Corinthians 15:20-22, 51-55, 58).

Our Hope of Heaven

May our struggles never cause us to lose the reality of the hope of heaven!

In Chapter Two, I wrote about Dyann Bennie's mother, Thelma (Grandma Thompson) who accepted Jesus just days before her death. It was the gift of a ceramic blue-bird from my wife, Carole, that broke Grandma's defenses, softening her heart to the Savior's voice. A few days later, at her memorial service, I read the following composition:

The Bluebird and the Angel

"It's a great morning; why are you here?"
Asked the bluebird of the angel.
"I've come to meet Grandma,
And to say, 'Never fear.'"

"It's a great morning; why are you here?"
Asked the angel of the bluebird.
"I've come to meet Grandma,
and to wipe away a tear.'"

So the two flew together
To meet their loved friend,
Saying, "Welcome to heaven,
Where your life will not end."

And they join us this morning,
Their wings full of flight,
To comfort, yes, remind us
That new hope brings new might.

For with the bluebird and the angel
Our dear Grandma would say,
"Walk on, weep no more;
It's a really great day."
—Ron Williams
August 23, 1994

Satisfied with God? Oh yes–to the fullest! He is life's highest delight!

Study Questions
Chapter 19 · Fully Satisfied

1. Review the promises and descriptions of Heaven throughout the writings of the New Testament.

2. How should the hope of Heaven and the promise of Jesus' return impact our daily living?

3. From 1 Corinthians 15, what are the benefits of Christ's resurrection?

4. How can we begin to view death as the "transformer" rather than the "terminator"?

5. How would you like to be remembered? (You are already writing your epitaph.)

BIBLIOGRAPHY

Hayford, Jack W., ed. *The Spirit Filled Life Bible.* Nashville: Thomas Nelson Publishers, 1991.

Lowery, Mark. *Out of Control.* Dallas: Word Publishers, 1996.

Moody, John. "A Vision of Judgment." *Time,* Dec. 20, 1993, pp. 58-61.

Shelley, Rubel. *In Step With the Spirit.* Grand Rapids, Mich.: Baker Book House, 1986.

Spurgeon, Charles H. *The Treasury of David.* 3 vols. Peabody, Massachusetts: Hendrickson Publishers, n.d.